HOW
WINNING
WORKS

HOW
WINNING
WORKS

8 ESSENTIAL LEADERSHIP LESSONS FROM THE TOUGHEST TEAMS ON EARTH

Robyn Benincasa

HOW WINNING WORKS

ISBN-13: 978-0-373-89255-6

Benincasa, Robyn.
How Winning Works: 8 essential leadership lessons from the toughest teams on earth/Robyn Benincasa
      p. cm.
ISBN 978-0-373-89255-6
1. Teams in the workplace. 2. Leadership. I. Title.
HD66.B4442 2012
658.4'092—dc23
          2011039910

www.Harlequin.com

Printed in U.S.A.

To Jeff Akens, the best soul mate ever,

who has dragged our stinky socks and moldy gear boxes

around every continent on Earth for the last fifteen years,

bless his amazing little MacGyver heart.

He has never, ever let me down.

And to my parents,

who believed in me beyond reason.

CONTENTS

INTRODUCTION

RAID GAULOISES ECUADOR
SEPTEMBER 1998
COTOPAXI VOLCANO
15,000 FEET

It was almost one o'clock in the morning. For four hours we had huddled together inside a hut perched 15,000 feet up the side of the Cotopaxi volcano, resting and preparing to make the final five-thousand-foot push to the summit. My teammates—Robert Nagle, John Howard, Ian Adamson and Steve Gurney—were snoring peacefully beside me, but I had not been able to stop crying since we entered the hut. I cried because it was the only way I could get oxygen, and I cried because I thought I was going to die if I had to climb higher.

We, Team Salomon-Presidio, had been running for three days at 14,000 feet on only two hours of sleep, and we were in the lead when we stumbled into this particular transition area, followed closely by the French team. On our arrival, the doctors and race organizers took one look at us and ordered both teams into a hut to lie down for a few hours, with neither team allowed to begin the summit push until 1:00 a.m. The altitude had clearly taken its toll on everyone. We were in bad shape, and I was one of the worst. All

I could do was take tiny sips of air. I was turning blue from lack of oxygen, and now we were about to attempt to summit this 19,700-foot soaring volcano, which is normally a weeklong mountaineering trip. It was the most extreme and audacious challenge in the history of adventure racing, a goal beyond reason or mercy, right in the middle of a nine-day nonstop expedition race that began at 14,000 feet with a seventy-five-mile run in subfreezing temperatures.

For safety's sake, the organizers decided to test everyone's oxygen saturation level before letting us climb higher. If a racer's oxygen level was less than seventy percent, they would not be allowed to continue, and the team would be charged a five-hour penalty. For the teams that could continue, there would be another checkpoint at 18,000 feet, and if any team member couldn't continue past that point, they'd be assessed a two-hour penalty and would have to go back down the hill with their tails between their legs. At the end of the day, however, at least three people would have to make it to the summit, or the entire team would be disqualified from the race.

So an oxygen saturation level of seventy percent was the magic number, the number that was going to mean the difference between winning and losing, and perhaps even between living and dying. I'm an emergency medical technician in my real-world job as a firefighter, so I understood the dangers of low oxygen saturation. It's a big red flag if you're at ninety-five percent or below. If your oxygen level is at eighty, you're nearly at death's door. Anything below ninety percent means we're rushing you to the hospital as a Code 3 with lights and sirens. So seventy percent seemed like a swell idea. I'd never seen anyone that low on our monitor who could still stand (and cry), so I reasoned that that couldn't be me.

Suddenly the doctor and race organizers appeared in the hut's doorway with the oxygen monitor, and everyone lined up to get their reading. One by one, each racer stuck an index finger into a clamp on the device, and a few seconds later, the doctor announced each result: "Ninety.... Eighty-eight.... Eighty-seven.... Ninety-two." Everyone was being cleared to continue, but I was the last one in line because I was afraid.

"If you're under seventy percent, we can't let you continue," the doctor said as he motioned to me to step forward.

I nodded. My hands were shaking as I pulled off my glove and exposed a finger so he could attach the clamp that would read my oxygen level.

John, Robert, Ian and Steve hovered, awaiting the results. I continued to shake.

"Seventy-one percent," the doctor said, shaking his head. He was at a loss for words. The glow of the number on the monitor spoke volumes: leave this hut, and you may not make it back. I had never been so afraid in my life. These elevations were too much to handle for a girl from sea level. I knew that racing with the best team in the world in a high-altitude race was a ridiculous plan, but I had hoped against hope that I would be good enough. Now those hopes were dashed by my failing lungs and my failing body. But a tiny speck of hope still lingered. Against all odds, I was still standing with seventy-one-percent oxygen saturation. How long can the human body endure this state? I wasn't too sure I wanted to find out.

I looked at my teammates, hoping one of them would pipe up and say, "Hey, it's not worth the risk. You stay here in this nice warm hut, and we'll take the five-hour penalty." But none of them said that. They just stood there in silence, waiting for me to decide. These guys were my heroes. They were legends in the sport, and I had been following their racing careers since starting my own in 1994. When they selected me to be their mandatory female teammate for this race, I jumped so high off my couch that I hit my head on my living room ceiling. This was the big time. This was my chance to prove myself; to show my heroes that they made the right choice in picking me for their team. The last thing I wanted to do was let them down. I made my decision.

"Guys, can you hook me up to the ropes and pull me up to eighteen?" I asked. "That way we'll only get a two-hour penalty."

So that was the plan we came up with. I'm not saying that it was a smart plan, or even a good plan, but as John always said, "At least it's a plan." Steve, John, Ian and Robert were literally going to drag my half-dead body another three thousand feet up the side of Cotopaxi on a rope attached to my climbing harness, and then they would leave me and continue on to the top so we could stay in the race.

Before I knew it, I was rigged for glacier travel, and we were on our way, climbing into the snowy darkness. Because I was the weakest link, I was put in the middle of the pack so if I went down, my teammates in front and behind could dig in with their ice axes and hold position. I don't remember anything except being petrified. Everything is much more intense and scary when you can't breathe. Not being able to move under my own power and being forced to rely so completely on other people was terrifying. We spent the whole night navigating glaciers, blinded by driving wind and snow, ascending upward at a snail's pace. As the sun rose and a new day dawned on Cotopaxi, I looked up and saw a group of people up ahead, waiting for us.

We had made it to 18,000 feet.

The five of us fell to our knees when we reached the checkpoint. I covered my face with my hands and cried. My body rocked with the wind gusts that swirled around me like tiny tornadoes. My only thought was about how in the world I would be able to get back down the mountain without my teammates, who were going to continue on to the summit without me. There I was, stuck halfway up the side of the mountain without an ounce of energy or water remaining, and I was about to be left alone. What was I going to do, slide down on my butt? Were they just going to push me and let me roll down?

And that's when Ian came up to me and said, "You ready?"

"But how am I going to get down?" I asked. I cried into my gloves.

"Down? Oh, I guess nobody told you yet. You're going up. It's just you, me and Steve now."

At that, I took my face out of my gloves, in which I had been hiding to try to escape the fear, the pain, the fact that I was clinging to life precariously on the side of an active volcano. I looked up to see that I was surrounded by television cameras. There was a large, black lens focusing on my face, filming my reaction to Ian's news. I tried to ignore the cameraman and focus on Ian, on getting my oxygen-starved brain to make sense of what he was saying, on making my body move with something other than involuntary shudders. Then I felt a hand on my shoulder. It was Robert.

"The doctor is not letting John and me go on, something about high-altitude pulmonary edema," he said with a wan smile.

"Listen to me. You have to go. You can do this. I know you can do this."

I know you can do this. Until the moment I heard those words, I was nothing but a scared little girl from San Diego who was just hoping not to screw up her team too much. But in that life-altering moment, when I heard those words and looked into Robert's eyes and saw that he truly believed I could get to the summit of Cotopaxi for the team, and I saw my teammates slowly but confidently nodding in agreement, I became a world champion adventure racer. The best racers on Earth had confidence in me, and they weren't just throwing me a bone. My teammates' belief in me changed not only my psychology but also my physiology, on the spot. Their faith transformed me. One minute I was on my knees in the snow with my head down, crying into my hands, and the next minute I was looking toward the top of the mountain and nodding yes, yes, yes.

I sank a couple of inches into the deep snow as I struggled to my feet. I felt hands grab me by my arms and help me stand. The cameras followed my every move.

"I can do it," I declared. And I would, despite the fact that I couldn't feel my legs or hands anymore, and despite the fact that the first stages of pneumonia were settling into my lungs. I had a fever of 104 and was coughing up green, spongy stuff that strangely looked like puzzle pieces. But I would continue. I would clip the rope tying my remaining two teammates and me to my climbing harness, pull my glacier glasses down over my eyes, cinch up my hood and climb those remaining 1,700 feet—for Robert and John, for the sick and scared weak link of a girl I was leaving behind at 18,000 feet and for my team.

So Steve, Ian and I climbed. And we climbed and we climbed and we climbed, each in our own little world. We moved sideways with cross steps so our crampons could catch on the ice, up the steep, snow-covered slope at a rate of about ten steps per agonizing minute. Each of us had an ice axe in one hand and a trekking pole in the other, which allowed us to use what was left of our arm strength as our legs slowly failed. Ian was practically dragging me up the mountain, with Steve bringing up the rear. I tried to focus on each grueling, treacherous step, but my mind kept returning to my teammates. I was not going to let them down. I was not going to stumble. I was not going to fall. I was not going to stop. I was not going to quit.

I didn't allow myself to look up because I was too afraid of the disappointment of how far away the peak would be. Just one step at a time. And another, and another. But I have to lie down! No you don't . . . and another . . . don't let Robert and John down. Be strong. But I'm not. Yes, you are. The internal battle to take just one more step raged on for what seemed like an eternity. Morning became afternoon, and there was still more uphill climbing. The white in my peripheral vision was infinite and relentless. My face was burning from dehydration and the searing glare of the sun off the snow. It was heaven to be on the best team in the world, at the front of the toughest race on Earth, and it was hellish suffering beyond reason. This was the penultimate moment of the race, the moment in which you choose which emotional tattoo you get to live with for the rest of your life: triumph or regret. And for hours, I wouldn't know the answer.

At the very end of my rope, physically, spiritually and emotionally, I looked up to the sky for a sign that everything was going to be okay, for a sign that I would live and that the suffering would end. And there it was. The end of the white. The sun. A stunning blue sky. The peak. I still had more than a couple hundred agonizing feet to go, but I was going to make it. My teammates had trusted in me, and I hadn't disappointed them. They believed in me beyond reason, and that belief elevated me to the top of one of the highest peaks in the Andes after three nonstop days and nights of racing.

When we reached the checkpoint at exactly 19,730 feet, Ian, Steve and I put our arms around one another, forming a tiny circle of solidarity and support, with our heads touching in the center. In a silence that spoke volumes, we acknowledged the soul-crushing journey, our friends who had believed in us and a moment together at the top of the world that we would remember for the rest of our lives. I cried some more.

And then we turned around and went back down. This was still a race, after all, and there were 250 more miles to go.

After five more nonstop days of head-to-head competition with the French through the jungles of Ecuador on mountain bikes, whitewater rafts, kayaks and blistered feet, we crossed the finish line in nine days, seven hours and fifty-one minutes. We were the first-ever American team to win an international adventure race.

I learned many lessons from my first race with my heroes.

I learned it was easier to breathe when I cried, so I cried often and without shame.

I learned that a teammate's faith in you can propel you up any mountain.

I learned that winning requires an entirely different mind-set than not losing.

I learned that the best teams in the world share not only their strengths but also their weaknesses.

I learned that you don't inspire your teammates by showing them how amazing you are. You inspire them by showing them how amazing they are.

And I learned that when people leave their egos at the starting line in pursuit of a common goal and form a deep and genuine connection to one another along the way—otherwise known as human synergy—they create a beautiful and unstoppable force that can handle whatever the winds, the mountains, the rivers and the jungles throw their way.

****

I gained my perspective on the art of human synergy the old-fashioned way. It wasn't an enlightened journey into a new understanding of the collective good, but rather a muddy, sleep-deprived, leech-infested necessity. I wanted to win the biggest, baddest, most ludicrous multisport endurance races on Earth: the Raid Gauloises and the Eco-Challenge. The only way to accomplish that goal was to travel for six to ten nonstop days and nights as part of a mixed-gender team of four or five people, staying within fifty yards of one another the whole time and doing whatever it took—running, mountain biking, paddling, crawling, clawing, bushwhacking and sliding on the most remote mountain peaks, frozen bogs, steaming hot jungles, deadly rivers and brain-frying deserts on the planet—to get to a finish line that's up to one thousand miles away, using only maps, compasses and teamwork. When you're in the middle of the special kind of togetherness that is adventure racing, you're bound to learn a thing or two about human relations.

I came to adventure racing from a triathlon background in the early 1990s, which officially makes me the Grandmother of Adventure Racing, I think. I read about the Raid Gauloises in *Runner's World* and was instantly intrigued by a sport that relied less on negative splits and ripped abs than on wits, skill and the human spirit. As I read, I remember thinking, *That's what I'd be good at! Suffering with cool people!* My first race was the Raid Gauloises in 1994, and although we finished dead last, I was hooked for life.

Adventure racing is like a Rubik's Cube of athleticism, teamwork, problem-solving skills and sheer guts. If you're missing one of those essential elements, you're sunk. But when you have a team that has the ability to arrange the puzzle just right, it's a magical experience beyond description. When our team won the Eco-Challenge in Borneo and the Raid Gauloises in Ecuador, we didn't have the greatest strength or the fastest feet in the pack. What we did have was a unique ability to take care of one another, to solve problems by open discussion and brainstorming, to relinquish our egos and accept help, to embrace a democratic style of leadership and to hang on to the lead like rabid terriers, which created a human synergy that allowed us to become not only better athletes but also better people.

The beauty of adventure racing is that at the end of the race, you haven't merely conquered a difficult course and tested your personal limits; you've actually proven yourself in life's most important adventure: being a great human being. Adventure racing allows us to bring out the hero, the warrior, the healer, the leader and the compassionate friend in each of us. In a successful adventure racing endeavor, we are our best, most enlightened selves, and we can see that reflected in the eyes of our teammates throughout the race and beyond the finish line. This is the reason we all sign up for the world's most life-affirming races again and again. Yes, the places we go and the landscapes we see in this sport are often awe-inspiring, which is much of the reason we plunk down that first big entry fee. But somewhere "out there," as the challenge becomes too much for one tiny speck of a human being on the vast face of the planet to handle and we allow ourselves to experience the comfort and strength of silently sharing one heart and one mind with a handful of other human beings, we are transformed and become transcendent. It is in these moments that adventure racing becomes more of a spiritual experience than a sport, and one toward which we are inexorably drawn. Which leads to the eternal question for every one of us: When's the next race?

Adventure racing is not an athletic event. It's an interpersonal and physical odyssey that represents the ultimate in interdependence with the people around you. Just as in business and in life, you have small teams of men and women working together, struggling to get through a series of seemingly endless checkpoints, in search of a nearly impossible finish line, in constantly changing conditions, operating under ridiculous deadlines, with each team trying to do it better than any other team in the industry. If that doesn't mirror our everyday lives in business, I don't know what does. In my experience, it is a lack of teamwork skills that is responsible for a large percentage of the DNFs (did not finish) in adventure racing, and the same is true in business. According to a *Harvard Business Review* study, the corporate climate (how employees feel about their work environment and the way they are treated) is responsible for *at least one third of a company's bottom-line profitability.*[1] That's huge! So the ability to improve the corporate climate by enhancing teamwork capacity on the job is an essential career skill, and adventure racing is a perfect analogy for extreme team building in the business world. Now, we've all been on teams since we were little kids, and we've been on teams as adults, too—at our jobs, in our marriages, in our families and in our communities. For most people, teamwork in those contexts is simply striving side by side together toward a common goal. But in order to be successful consistently, *you must step beyond the boundaries of ordinary teamwork and into the powerful realm of human synergy.* Human synergy is like teamwork supersized. Human synergy means that as we strive together toward this common goal, we actually become better because of one another. I'm better, stronger, faster, more productive and more successful because you are by my side. I make you better. You make me better. When we achieve human synergy, the results of our efforts are far greater than anything we could have accomplished as individuals. We're not just walking side by side toward a common goal anymore. Sometimes we're actually carrying one another for the good of the team.

In the races that my team and I have won, we were able to consistently create that ephemeral quality or magic that is human synergy to make our team better than the collective training and experience of our individual members. Consistently is the operative word. One of my favorite quotes on this subject is from the great Vince Lombardi, who said:

---

1   Daniel Goleman, "Leadership That Gets Results," *Harvard Business Review* (March/April 2000): R00204.

> *"You don't do things right once in a while, you do them right all the time. Winning is a habit. Unfortunately, so is losing."*

I couldn't agree more. So much of what separates one team from another is not talent but the ability of each and every teammate to consistently create synergy. Once you understand how to generate synergy, you have a toolbox of effective skills to use in any situation and with any team, whether you're working on a short project with colleagues or a successful, lifelong marriage. If you make a habit of building and maintaining that synergy, you will make a habit of crossing every finish line that you set your mind to.

Human synergy—if I could bottle the stuff, I would be a billionaire. But after fifteen years of studying what causes a team to evolve from ordinary to extraordinary in the most extreme classrooms on Earth, I believe I've found the formula for creating a winning team builder within each of us. When the eight elements of that formula are lined up just right, they spell out one of my favorite words:

T*otal commitment.* Does your team have the Four Ps of Commitment: preparation, planning, purpose and perseverance?

E*mpathy and awareness.* Do you and your teammates care about one another as much as you care about yourselves? You must be able to put yourselves in one another's shoes often and give one another what you need, whether that's a pat on the back, a hug or a kick in the pants. Under all circumstances, treat one another the way you would want to be treated.

Adversity management. How does your team deal with a race that's not going well? You must remember that most races are generally a long series of problems to solve and not the straight-forward sprint you were hoping for. The right attitude is key. Does your team see adversity as a roadblock or a challenge? Are you ruled by the hope of success or the fear of failure? Do you let the pursuit of perfection hinder your progress?

Mutual respect. Is there a high level of trust, respect and loyalty within your team? Find things to love about your teammates while minimizing the things that bug you. Remember to appreciate the great skills and attitudes that each teammate brings to the table and believe in one another beyond reason.

We thinking. Are you constantly looking for ways to utilize your collective resources for the most successful outcome? "We thinking" is about bringing everyone across the finish line with you and not just being a standout player on your own. If you are the strong link, do you just happily enjoy yourself at the front of the pack, or do you stop and realize that feeling good means you should be carrying more weight for someone who is struggling?

Ownership of the project. Are you choosing the kind of team-mates who can wrap themselves around the team's mission? Are you helping people embrace the goals by allowing them to create those goals?

Relinquishment of ego. Are you willing to check your ego at the starting line for the good of the team? You will be your team's strongest link or its weakest link at one point or another. Your ego is the heaviest thing in your backpack, so don't let it get between you and the finish line.

Kinetic leadership. Is your team flexible enough to allow different leaders to emerge whenever the situation calls for it? Teammates should be encouraged to come forward whenever their strengths and experiences are the most useful. On the best teams, the leadership revolves constantly, as do leadership styles.

So there you have it: the Eight Essential Elements of Human Synergy. The rest of this book explains how to apply those elements to create synergy with every teammate every day, using examples of the good, the bad and the not so pretty in teamwork from this insane interpersonal petri dish called adventure racing. My goal is to mentor that team builder who lives inside of you so you can create world-class teams everywhere you go. Developing and maintaining a mind-set of yourself as a team builder has real staying power, whether you're strengthening an existing team at work or at home, or connecting with clients you associate with only a few times each year or even in a one-minute sales call. Those little tweaks in thinking allow you to consistently create win-win situations with the people around you. Here's what I know for sure: you don't get to the finish line with ego and bravado; you get there with humility, teamwork and grace. Isn't bringing everyone across the finish line with you at the end of the day a far more worthy and productive goal than just getting there first but alone?

That certainly has been the case for me. My team's most epic experiences in the outdoors were not about standing on the winner's podium but about the synergetic moments we shared on our way there. It's no coincidence that my memory banks for my racing career are full not of the places we went but of the human connections we achieved in our shared moments of fear, triumph, defeat and joy. Some of the most vivid memories are of the times when my teammates were my heroes, my coaches, my saviors—and of the times when they allowed me to be theirs.

Those moments of synergy, of mixing strength and weakness for the good of the team, of hurtling toward the next milestone as one mind and one heart, unencumbered by ego or reproach for weakness— those are the moments I wish for you and your team, you and your partner and kids, you and your colleagues, you and your neighbors. Let your teammates be your heroes. And have the courage to be theirs.

ELEMENT 1:

TOTAL COMMITMENT

"Everyone starts strong.
Success comes to those with unwavering commitment
to be at the end."

—Howard Schultz, CEO of Starbucks

How many times have you launched a project and had everybody show up on day one with their hair on fire, ready to go full blast, only to have their gusto and energy disappear the minute things start getting tough? My guess is you've seen that happen more times than you can count. Frustrating, isn't it?

If you expect to have a winning team, you and your teammates have to develop the first essential element of human synergy—total commitment—not only to the task at hand but also to one another. Here's a news flash: it's not always the strongest, fastest team that finishes first, but the team that is the most committed. Commitment doesn't start at the beginning of the race when everyone's all pumped up and chomping at the bit. *Commitment starts when the fun stops.* When you are no longer having a good time, your team's dedication, or the lack thereof, will spell the difference between victory and defeat.

There is a racer in our sport, Mike Kloser, who is a world champion of mountain biking and the poster child for total commitment. Because of his "never say die" attitude, Mike completely ruined adventure racing for everyone else. It was the late 1990s, and my teammates and I were motoring along, minding our own business, happily winning lots of races simply because we got out in front and people couldn't see us anymore. Then along came Mike to screw everything up. His attitude was "Until that team ahead of me crosses the finish line, they haven't beaten me," and he behaved accordingly, meaning he often came charging in from behind and kicked some unsuspecting team's collective butt. It was never over until it was over for Mike. Because of his undying commitment to excellence, he raised the bar for everyone. So I just had to get him onto my team because I decided that it would be a heck of a lot easier to join him than to beat him. I learned a long time ago that awesome athletes are everywhere but committed teammates like Mike Kloser are a rare breed indeed.

Mike and the other extreme athletes I've competed with and against over the years have taught me a thing or two about total commitment and how teams can develop and maintain that essential element through even the toughest of circumstances. Having that "it's not over until it's over" mentality, assembling the proper tools, defining what the end goal is and rallying your team around it is the formula for achieving total commitment. Let's take a closer look at the building blocks to total commitment, the Four Ps: preparation, planning, purpose and perseverance.

PREPARATION

We seldom succeed in the long run by winging it. Of course, we sometimes end up being forced to wing it because circumstances change, but coming to a race unprepared rarely leads to a strong finish. World-class extreme teammates know this, and they demonstrate their dedication to the end goals and to one another by being fully committed to pre-event preparation. Can you imagine what might happen if, in an adventure race or a desperate fire-and-rescue situation, one of your teammates decided to just hop up off the couch and show up without putting in the training time it takes to become his or her best? In business, we can sometimes fake our way through and get away with being underprepared. We've all done it. But being a member of an extreme team means that you come to the starting line in the best shape of your life and one hundred percent committed to the goal, even if achieving it means you have to crawl there with someone on your back. People are counting on you, and the bigger and more audacious the goal, the more important your preparation and ultimate contribution will be.

In the races we've won, each of the team members started in peak mental and physical condition and had nothing left at the finish line. We used up every spiritual and physical resource we had in the course of the race. If even one person had shown up in less than their absolute best shape, we wouldn't have been lying there on the finish line, gasping for air and sobbing, but victorious nonetheless.

Many people thought my teams were just lucky when we first started winning races, but we had a different definition of luck. To us, luck is the intersection where opportunity meets preparation.

Luck = Opportunity + Preparation

Without preparation, there is no luck. Opportunities come and go, but why wait passively for opportunity to knock when you can take control of the situation and create some for yourself? When you are fully prepared to capitalize on whatever comes along *and* able to generate a few opportunities for yourself, you become the luckiest person who ever lived.

One of the luckiest people I know is Steve Gurney, a New Zealand adventure racing champ. In the weeks leading up to the 2003 Lake Tahoe Primal Quest event, a 450-mile-long, five-day adventure race through the Sierras, Steve contacted the race director and asked for details about the kayaks that were going to be provided for the paddling segment. He wanted to know what type of boat it was and what all the measurements were. Unbeknownst to the race officials and his competitors, Steve had been doing some research and tinkering around with his kayaks at home, trying to figure out how to make them go faster. He discovered that the longer and thinner the boats were, the faster they would go. Based on the specs of the kayaks that we were going to be given to use in the Tahoe race, Steve designed and built this crazy nose cone contraption that he could fasten to the front of the Primal Quest kayak to stabilize and lengthen it by about five feet. I'm not sure if he built it on site in Nevada or had it shipped from New Zealand, but his crew had it waiting for him at the start of the paddling section. As "luck" would have it, Steve's invention worked like a charm. By the end of the first leg, his team was at least an hour ahead of the next closest boat and well on its way to winning.

Everybody in that race had blindly accepted that we had to use the boats as is, that we would have to do the best we could with what we had. Everybody, that is, except that lucky devil, Steve Gurney. He turned the whole race on its ear and said, "Why do I have to use only the tools they give me? Why can't I make what we've got better? There's no rule that says I can't."

That's the kind of lateral thinking that wins sporting events—and contracts and clients and sales. If the rules don't prohibit it, then it's fair game. Why resign yourself to the parameters and just run the race as it's laid out for you? When you're totally prepared to create your own game and do it better than anyone else out there, that's the kind of thinking and behavior that makes you a world-class leader and an extreme teammate like Steve Gurney.

That's also the kind of thinking that made my racing buddy, New Zealand's John Howard, the most decorated adventure racer throughout the 1990s. John was a consistent winner because he was a pro at making sure his team always had viable options from which to choose. He was the King of Options. One of us would show up with a certain kind of ice axe or a particular type of snowshoe or a standard piece of climbing gear and be satisfied with that, but John would never settle for it. He knew that what was required to succeed in the moment was not always what the team originally thought it would need, so he always brought a wide variety of tools. That way we could choose the best one for the changing conditions each and every time. Other teams didn't give themselves the luxury of options. Expecting snow, they'd be content to pack their snowshoes, and then out in the middle of nowhere, they'd discover that the snow was actually more like ice and what they really needed was crampons. And they'd be moving like pond scum. But because of John and his options, his teams were always ready for anything. John understood that change is the only thing you can count on in racing, in business and in life. Standing at the base of a soaring mountain with the right tool for that particular job in that particular moment makes all the difference in the world.

Which brings me back to Mike Kloser. Along with John Howard, Mike is one of the most victorious guys in the sport. In addition to his "never say die" attitude, Mike was "lucky" for a couple of additional reasons, both having to do with preparation. First, he trained scientifically. If he was going to be running an altitude race, he went to that altitude two weeks ahead of time. If he was going to be in a heat race, he jumped around in the sauna for two months before the event. Few others demonstrated that kind of total commitment.

The second reason Mike excelled was the condition of his gear. Each competitor has a gear box containing his or her personal equipment—things like batteries, climbing gear, headlamps, ice axes, bike shoes, helmets and medicine. You pack your own box, and then your crew brings it out whenever you get to a transition area. You sit down, have a little something to eat, warm up or cool off, stow your stuff from the last leg in your gear box and get out your stuff for the next leg. If everyone on your team does this correctly, then you should be in and out of transition in around twenty minutes. But if your gear box is disorganized to begin with, or if you throw your old wet clothes from this leg on top of your old wet clothes from the last leg, then by the end of the race, it's an absolute train wreck in there. Your brain is fried from exhaustion, and you can't find anything you need because you didn't take the time to prepare and organize your gear box properly. Don't ask me how I know this. In the transition area, my nickname was Yard Sale for a reason.

But then there was Mike Kloser. He was so much cleaner than everyone else with his transitions, figuratively and literally. Before the race, he took the time to create little drawers and containers that were exactly the right size for each piece of gear, with everything appropriately labeled and perfectly laid out inside.

Mike was always the first one ready to leave transition. He was always the one who knew where his stuff was, and he was always the one who didn't forget anything. I'd be whining about losing a headlamp, searching in vain through the wreckage that was my gear box, and invariably Mike would say in this matter-of-fact tone, "Well, I've got one right here, in the appropriately labeled headlamp pouch. Take it."

Mike understood that the extra preparation he went through before the race might seem unnecessary or excessive at the time, but he also understood that our minds were not going to work properly in the heat of battle. He knew that if he could keep himself somewhat organized, he would be able to get himself and his teammates through the race so much more cleanly. Instead of digging around in his box in the middle of the night, he was going to know exactly where his batteries, his gloves and his spare bike chain were. Mike was never the one holding up his team. He was never the problem because he always showed up one hundred percent ready to go. He believed that preparation was going to be one of the keys to his racing success, and he was right. We, his eternally grateful teammates, appreciated that, even though we teased him about it.

We also appreciated native Australian Ian Adamson and his glorious way with maps. In adventure racing, you receive your course maps about twenty-four hours before the race. These maps aren't like your grandpa's Rand McNally road atlas. They consist of about thirty huge maps that you have to lay out end to end so you can see the entire seven-day course and plot each checkpoint along the way to figure out the quickest route to each one. Every team has its own recipe for how they handle these maps. The least prepared teams would plot the checkpoints and decipher the route to the first few, firm in their belief that they could then figure out the rest on the fly. Then they'd head to bed to rest up for the next day's start.

But not Ian Adamson. Not only did he plot all the checkpoints from start to finish but also, with our help, he took the time to chart our course for the entire race. Then he would write tips and hints in the map's margins, noting different things that we ought to be aware of along the way: what this checkpoint was going to look like, how many degrees it was going to be off that last meadow—all the tiny details your brain needs to have spelled out for it when you're sleep-deprived and starving. But Ian was still not done. Once he had everything plotted and noted on the maps, he painstakingly laminated them with contact paper to make them water-resistant, and he filed them away according to his own special system.

It took eighteen to twenty hours to complete those maps to Ian's satisfaction. Typically we'd only get a couple hours of sleep before heading to the starting line, but it ended up being worth it. Here's the thing with adventure racing: just like in life and business, you always assume that you'll have plenty of time to tackle a chore tomorrow, but then something unexpected happens, and you can't do it—or you lose your map. Thanks to Ian's spectacular commitment to preparation, we'd be motoring along with all the confidence in the world because we knew exactly where we were and where we were headed. We'd see all these other teams standing along the trail fighting about their maps and whose pack they were in and who lost them and why is this one wet. As we blew by those "unlucky" racers time after time, we realized that the teams that win these races are not necessarily the ones that are going the fastest but the ones that have to slow down the least. We came to the conclusion that if we have our ducks in a row and we make good decisions and take care of each other, we're going to win a bunch of races because we're not intimidated by the super-fast teams anymore.

Just like in life and business, in an adventure race we have a general idea of what is expected of us. We understand the specific competencies we bring to the table as teammates, but we don't know the actual layout of the race until just before it starts. And that's okay, because you and your world-class teammates are going to show up prepared to handle anything that comes your way. In my definition, a world-class team doesn't necessarily need to know how to handle *everything;* it just needs to be built with people who are prepared to handle *anything.*

PLANNING

You've come to the starting line prepared. You've been given a map, and your goal has been laid before you. But before you set out on your epic journey in pursuit of that goal, it's first things first: it's time to develop a plan. Management consultant Peter Drucker once wrote,

"Plans are only good intentions unless they immediately degenerate into hard work." So how do you get beyond vague intentions and actually make some great things happen for your team?

- **Chart your course.** Sit down with your map and plot the entire route to your destination. Think about where you are now and envision where you ultimately want to end up.

- **Decide your pacing.** Pacing is something that's often over-looked in business. Much of the time we just operate on a low, day-to-day hum, hoping to eventually end up where we want to go. Or sometimes we get an exciting new goal and come out of the blocks with our hair on fire, only to burn out because we can't sustain that level of intensity for long. I'm a big fan of identifying the little hills that you really want to charge up when you come to them—where you most want to make your impact and where you want to push hard—because if you don't have a plan for where you want to dedicate your greatest energy and where you want to rest, then you'll either come on too strong and burn out, or not go hard enough and fall short. You have to find a sustainable pace for the long haul.

- **Set interim checkpoints.** When I worked for a pharmaceutical company, my manager gave me my year-end sales goal and then walked away, assuming that I would somehow eventually meet that goal with minimal information to gauge my progress. That's like a race director giving each team a map and a compass and saying, "You're not going to be sure if you're on the right track or what your progress is for the entire ten-day race, but whoever gets to the finish line first wins. See you in a thousand miles." People would be so demoralized after only two or three days that they'd never make it to the end.

The only thing that saved us was having checkpoints along the way. A thousand-mile race didn't seem nearly as impossible when all we had to do was get to the next checkpoint and then the next checkpoint and then the next. It's intimidating for your team to be told that in three years you want to be the number one company in your industry and then leave them with no way of knowing along the way if they're on track to achieve the goal. Make sure your people know what their weekly, monthly and quarterly goals are so they can chart their progress. That's what motivates teams to keep going.

> "PLANS ARE ONLY GOOD INTENTIONS UNLESS THEY IMMEDIATELY DEGENERATE INTO HARD WORK."
> —Peter Drucker

Now let's talk about planning versus execution. Sometimes people are so paralyzed by planning and the false sense it brings of being productive that they never get to work. I've seen fire captains, racing teams and business leaders plan and plan and plan to death while the house burns down, or the other team breezes by and takes the lead, or a business opportunity is lost to an alert competitor. On the flip side are the people who roll up their sleeves and wing it at high speed without giving it a second thought. I've seen racers spring into action off a starting line and just follow the pack, having never even looked at their maps, and I've watched firefighters run into a burning building alone with no partner or plan at all, hoping to be a big hero. Neither scenario ended well.

Clearly the best practice lies somewhere in between the two extremes of over- and underplanning. There are obvious considerations, such as how much time you have for planning versus the immediacy of the situation. But in general, the most successful teams naturally opt for a solid mix of planning and execution, realizing that most projects are fluid and require continuous feedback and reassessment. In the fire service, the majority of commanders utilize some version of what I call the STRAP plan to effectively manage that process of feedback and reassessment. STRAP is a tool that anyone can use to create a sound plan and turn it into a course of action that gets winning results. Of note here is how far down in the plan the action is.

Size up the scene. Exactly what is going on here? I see smoke, but where is the fire? What are the dangers? A good team leader always walks around and assesses all six sides of the building. Don't try to evaluate from only one angle.

Tactical priorities are established. What is my most important outcome? In order of priority, is it rescue, protecting neighboring homes, confining the blaze to one area, extinguishing the fire or salvaging whatever we can?

Resources needed. Do we have everything it takes to be successful in this mission? Do I need to call in more units or specialty personnel, or get a rescue team in place to help any firefighters who might become trapped?

Action! Now, go and attack the fire!

Position, progress and needs (PPN). The chief continually asks the leaders on the fire—the captains—for their PPN. What is your status, how is your progress and what other resources do you need to complete the job? Then the chief continually reassesses and recalculates his or her STRAP plan based on all of the incoming PPN reports from the field.

By using a STRAP plan system, the leader avoids getting stuck in assessment mode and also ensures that the most important variables are considered and properly addressed as the situation changes.

The final essential phase of planning, which is actually an advance planning exercise for the next challenge, is the all-important debrief. Trust me, as a firefighter and teammate who is generally low on the chain-of-command totem pole of life, I know that when some-

> "THE MOST SUCCESSFUL TEAMS NATURALLY OPT FOR A SOLID MIX OF PLANNING AND EXECUTION."

one says the word *debrief,* what we hear is the word *inquisition,* and we start sweating. But as a leader, you must make it clear that this is not an assessment of blame or an opportunity for finger-pointing or criticism. It is the foundation for the next plan, and it is intended to make the company and the team stronger. Then, facilitate the debrief with that intention. Conduct it as soon as you can after the task. In addition to giving your feedback, ask your team members for theirs. In other words, listen—*really* listen.

Two excellent questions to ask each person during debriefing are, what are the top one or two things you learned from this task? and what might we consider doing differently next time? That way, you're allowing your teammates to discover their own answers and arrive at their own truths without being pressured into seeing it your way. People need to be able to walk away from debriefing feeling as if they have contributed to the common good. They need to feel as if their experience and input were valued and not feel like they've been raked over the coals. So keep the session honest, direct and positive, and you'll all come out of it more committed than ever and with a jump start on your next big adventure.

The bottom line is that even though we can't possibly have all the answers at the beginning of any worthwhile journey, successful teams know that planning is essential to a healthy start. But extremely successful teams take it a step further and understand that the planning doesn't end once the journey has begun. As the leader of an extreme team, your PPN must be a continuous loop for the duration.

PURPOSE

We are all in business to do well, but most of us also want to do good. We want to be a part of something larger than ourselves. We want to feel as if we're contributing, to feel like we're being recognized for our talents, to have the opportunity to shine and to have our experience valued. A great teammate consistently helps people inspire themselves by elevating their sense of purpose. This is especially important when things get tough and people are losing their will to go on. In my experience, teams either quit or find a reason to continue based on the emotional intelligence of their leaders. The leader's ability not only to read his or her team members and pick up on what they need but also to find a way for them to still win—in essence, to restructure the vision of what winning is—is critical to the team's success.

For example, everyone starts out with a goal. For some it's simply to win. For others it's to break into the top ten. And for still others, it's just to cross that finish line. Somewhere along the way, those hopes get dashed by challenging circumstances (this race is longer and harder than we imagined), a lack of preparation (major heatstroke because someone came from a New Zealand winter to race in Death Valley), acts of God (the river gets too high to cross), or whatever the case may be. You can't win 'em all. Or can you? Great leaders will reframe what a win looks like to appeal to the higher self of each of their teammates and to motivate them through the dark void of disappointment. Consistently instilling a sense of common purpose to mobilize the team and creating a rally point and phrases to inspire through a greater good is what a world-class team leader does.

One of my favorite adventure racers and business leaders, a friend named David Kelly, is a wizard when it comes to the "reframe and refocus" strategy. I can't tell you how many times I've heard him say things like, "Hey guys, we're not winning, but we're *clearly* in contention for a top-five finish here!" Then later, "We're clearly in contention for a top-ten finish here, guys! How cool would it be to be a top-ten team of the Eco-Challenge?" Or this: "Let's make our families and sponsors proud and show 'em a team with more guts than any other team in this race!" That's David, always finding a way for his teammates to reach, to elevate, to win.

When our bicycles didn't show up at the last leg of the Raid Gauloises in Tibet, we were body-slammed with the terrible realization that after leading for five agonizing, heart-wrenching, twenty-four-hour days, carefully building our lead at up to 17,000 feet of pulmonary edema–inducing altitude, we might lose the race. On top of that was the bleak reality of sitting on our butts in an open field while every other team in the race rode by to stare at our tear-streaked faces and pity our fate while gleefully moving up a place in the rankings. Ugh! To this day, I still shudder just thinking of it. But the main thing I remember was the lifeline our team captain, Robert Nagle, threw to my dying spirit. "Great leaders reframe what a win looks like. We are the world champions, and now we're going to prove why. *Nothing* will stop us," he declared. And suddenly my heart was racing.

> **"GREAT LEADERS REFRAME WHAT A WIN LOOKS LIKE."**
> —Robert Nagle

The tears stopped flowing. There was a gauntlet thrown down by this race, and we were going to answer with a loud, resounding collective voice that required no sound, only action. The world champions are here, and it's time to show the world who we are. Our win is no longer tied to crossing the finish line first. Our win is tied to our character as a team. Just like that, Robert elevated our sense of purpose, gave us a new way to win and redirected our emotional course with only a few well-placed words.

So, how did the Tibet race turn out, you ask? You're going to have to keep reading to find out!

PERSEVERANCE

World-class team members know that the mountain is always going to be higher, the river is always going to be wider, the course is always going to be longer, the terrain is always going to be rockier, and completing the task at hand is always going to be another inch away, no matter how close you get. It's a mind-set that keeps you sane. Assume the worst and work frantically toward the best, but never, ever, ever give up. Because the moment you do, you often discover that relief (for example, the next checkpoint, the top of the hill, the end of the freezing cold whitewater swimming section, the first ray of sunlight or the FDA approval you've been waiting for) was right around the next corner. It happens all the time.

Sometimes hope is all you have left, and you must be unwavering in your patience and faith all the way to the finish line no matter how difficult it may be. Because guess what? Your competition surely is.

If I had to choose the one race that most tested my team's commitment to perseverance, it would be the 1995 Raid Gauloises in Argentina. Just thinking about it hurts my brain. It was a 300-mile race through Patagonia that included everything from hiking to climbing to kayaking to horseback riding. I was racing with my Kiwi boys—Neil Jones, Jeff Mitchell and Chris Morrissey—and we were running in the top five, desperately trying to catch Mike Kloser and his friends at the front of the pack. There was a huge mountain climb about three fourths of the way through the race. It was a searing hot one hundred degrees at the base of the mountain. We started climbing, and the higher we climbed, the colder it got. Pretty soon it was snowing, and before long we were in full whiteout conditions with massive accumulations.

Unfortunately, we only had our lighter weight jackets with us; nobody had predicted that kind of unseasonable snowstorm. We trudged onward as darkness fell. Our mission was to find the checkpoint at the peak, then navigate another eight hours' worth of switchbacks all the way down to the transition area on the other side, where we would jump into kayaks for the final leg.

But when we arrived at the peak, we couldn't find the checkpoint. We wandered around and around, but there was no sign of it. Jeff and Chris, who both had really low body fat, became dangerously hypothermic. They were stumbling, staring and trying to lay down to sleep. Neil went out into the darkness to look for signs of the checkpoint and left me to keep our teammates awake. The snow was building up all around us. Both Jeff and Chris had lost the ability to speak or respond to me in any way. I'd get eye contact when I shook them, and I could see they were trying to think through what I wanted them to do, but they simply weren't there anymore. Had I walked away, they would have both gone to sleep, and that would have been the end. I was nearly frantic. I was shaking them to keep them awake and laying on them to provide some warmth when Neil came back an hour later with the horrible news that he still could not find the checkpoint. It simply wasn't there.

Four teams eventually gathered there, all of us lost and unable to find the checkpoint. We bonded together to take care of the dangerously hypothermic racers on each of our teams while the stronger ones fanned out in search of this elusive checkpoint. But when two hours had passed and we still hadn't found it, we decided that we had to go down to the transition area regardless. We reasoned that the checkpoint person had probably descended because of the storm.

Screw the race; people were about to die up here. Surely the race director would understand that if four of the top teams couldn't find the checkpoint, then there was a fatal flaw in the race. We shook our teammates awake, made them drink some fluids with electrolytes and calories to help them generate body heat, put them on towlines, and dragged them down the mountain for hours. All four teams stumbled down the mountain together on a group survival mission, with all thoughts of racing left far behind us in the deep snow that nearly claimed our teammates.

We arrived at base camp eight hours later, at the dawn of a new day. The sixteen of us looked as if we had just come off Mount Everest. Our faces were deeply wrinkled and drawn from dehydration. Our skin was red, mottled and cracking from the high-altitude sun exposure, our eyes ringed black from complete exhaustion. We looked like extras from *Dawn of the Dead* as we approached the transition area, just staring, unfeeling, completely depleted of every ounce of energy and sanity. My fiancé and crew captain, Jeff Akens, came running, and we asked for immediate medical help for our teammates. We told him all about the missing checkpoint, too, but we didn't really care about that anymore. We were sure the officials would shut down the race because there had been such a terrible breach, but one sentence from Jeff slammed us back into the real world.

"Well, the two teams in front of you found the checkpoint," he said, "and the race organizers are saying you have to find it, too, or you'll be disqualified."

This couldn't be happening! Not only were we not going to get medical help, but we were also going to be disqualified? People nearly died up there! How could they not know or care about what we had just been through? The truth was that they didn't. On both counts.

Apparently what had happened was that Checkpoint Guy unknowingly set up his tent in the wrong place, about a half mile from where he was supposed to be. The first two teams arrived at the peak before dark, so they could see the smoke from a fire that Checkpoint Guy had built to stay warm, and that smoke led them in. By the time we got up there, Checkpoint Guy had already put out his fire and sought the shelter of his tent, leaving no light for us and no signal fire to indicate where he was. This was clearly an issue with the race and not with our navigation. The checkpoint was in the wrong place and had no signal lights. How could we be held accountable for that?

All four teams went together to meet with the race officials and explain what happened. We were sure they'd be sympathetic to our plight. But they told us that because the checkpoint had indeed been up there and the other two teams ahead of us had found it, we would be disqualified if we failed to reach it. In other words, we had to climb the mountain again or forfeit. The sixteen of us stood there in jaw-dropping disbelief. We were six days into that race. We'd been through the horror of our lives, nearly losing our teammates in a whiteout at 14,000 feet, and instead of an apology and blankets and food and medical care for our hypothermic teammates, we were told, "Sorry, but if you don't reach the checkpoint, you'll be disqualified."

In retrospect, this moment was such a vivid reminder that nobody else can ever really walk in your shoes or live in your world or be in your head. Every human interaction is a clash of realities. In this case, we had just lived through a life-altering, life-threatening mountaineering odyssey. In the race director's world, from a warm tent next to a lake with dinner service at his disposal, we missed a checkpoint. I think of this moment often, whenever I experience a misunderstanding with someone. Maybe this is just a reality clash and a moment to discover the reality that this person is operating from versus assuming my reality is the only one that exists. These race directors were not only coming from a separate reality but also speaking from a completely different galaxy far, far away. They didn't care what we'd been through, and they weren't open to hearing what we had to say about the misplaced checkpoint. They only cared about their rules. In the real world, these guys would not have been running a successful company.

"EVERY HUMAN INTERACTION IS A CLASH OF REALITIES."

So we had a horrible decision to make. Did we come all the way to Argentina only to have to go home and tell our sponsors and families and everybody else that we didn't finish the race? Or do we go through the hell of climbing that mountain all over again? It was an agonizing decision—so agonizing, in fact, that two of the four teams told the race officials to shove it and disappeared into their tents. But we and an Argentinean team decided that we had to go back. Sure, it was Checkpoint Guy's error that put us in that predicament, but it would have done us no good to stand around blaming him. It was still our race to run. We would not quit.

It took fifteen hours to make our second round-trip, to hike all the way up that snowy mountain to find the checkpoint, only to turn around and go back down again. It was five hundred times harder to reach our goal than we ever dreamed it would be. But I knew if we made it through that hell, we would have one more beautiful brick to add to our Character Walls, and we would be able to keep it forever and ever.

The most addictive thing about stretching yourself the way we did that day is the realization that you *can* go farther and you *can* endure more and you *can* keep putting one foot in front of the other. In adventure racing, we not so jokingly refer to this as excellent suffering, and coming through it makes you even stronger and more durable the next time you're challenged. It's like in business, when you stay up all night working on a report when you'd really like to be doing something else. You work until 4:00 a.m., but you know it's perfect, and you know you've expelled every ounce of effort you could into it. When you go further than you ever thought you could, it's a life-altering experience, and you come out on the other side with greater confidence. I think most people never know how much they're capable of because they don't hang in there long enough to find out.

One person I know who always hangs in there is Isaac Wilson, one of my teammates for the 2000 Borneo Eco-Challenge. That kid was like Charlie Brown: if something bad was going to happen to anyone, it was going to happen to poor Isaac. At around day three of the Borneo race, we were in the lead and hauling butt on one of the long jungle hiking sections. When you're the lead team on a jungle trail in Borneo, you never know what you're going to run into. We literally ran into a herd of elephants on our mountain bikes once. Yes, literally. That's part of the joy (and fear) of being first on the trail. But on this particular day, our team's lead runner kicked up a wasp's nest that was on the ground. The second and third runners just further pissed off the wasps, and the fourth runner? Yep, it was Isaac, and he got nailed. The wasps were all over him. He started screaming, waving his arms around like a madman and running down the trail inside this huge cloud of irate wasps until he finally escaped them. He was stung about twenty times. It was terribly painful, but the stinging was only the beginning. Once the venom kicked in, Isaac began this blood-curdling screaming that I will never forget.

"It feels like my brain is going to explode!" he shrieked as he walked around holding his head. There we were, leading this race, and if we had been in the real world, Isaac would have been on his way to the emergency room. We had him sit down for a couple minutes while we tried to console him, but sitting seemed to make it worse. For the next three hours, we walked beside our teammate while he held his head and screamed this crazy anguished scream, but it never slowed him down. He just kept walking and screaming. Isaac chose to walk on in agony rather than sit still in agony. He was going to be in agony no matter what, so why not win a race while he was at it? And we did.

****

So tell me, are you as committed as Isaac to your personal and professional goals? Or do you frequently let yourself off the hook because it seems easier to do that than to follow through when the going gets tough? Do you catch yourself making excuses for why you can't or don't need to go on, even when you know in your heart that you can? Do you hear yourself at around 4:00 p.m. saying, "Ah, that's enough for today. It's getting too dark, too cold, too hot, too humid, too (fill in the blank), and I'm tired because I worked out yesterday; so I'll finish this tomorrow?"

If that sounds like you and your team, pledge today to become better prepared, to formulate a plan, to find a renewed sense of purpose and to persevere tomorrow. That way, the next time the fun stops—and oh, yes, the fun most certainly will stop at some point—your total commitment to excellence will kick in and carry you through, no matter how grueling your race may be.

Whenever people ask me what in the world motivated me to stand at the finish line of more than thirty-five of the most ridiculous, backbreaking multisport races on Earth, my truthful answer goes something like this:

> When I'm at the end of my rope, shivering, crying, afraid and empty, I picture myself sitting in my backyard two weeks from then, warm and comfortable, watching the sunset and drinking a glass of wine with my favorite people around me, with this incredible journey behind me and holding in my heart and mind the sense of accomplishment of standing there at the finish line, emotionally and physically spent, in tatters, but with my team around me and with memories of victory and defeat that will last a lifetime. And then I think of the alternative, of sitting there in my backyard full of regrets and questions, second-guessing my character, analyzing my weaknesses and wondering if my teammates will ever ask me to race with them again. Then I decide in that moment which reality I want to live with.
>
> And I keep walking.

TOTAL COMMITMENT:
A BUSINESS CASE STUDY

For their bestselling book *Built to Last: Successful Habits of Visionary Companies,* authors Jim Collins and Jerry Porras studied companies that have prospered for at least one hundred years, and compared them with competitors that haven't fared as well. Collins and Porras found that the winning companies all have an overarching ideology that directs the actions of everyone in the company from the top down. Only those people who demonstrate total, ongoing commitment to the company's core values are allowed to be part of the team.

No matter what your team's specific mission is, you increase the odds of accomplishing it when you motivate your teammates to first pledge their total commitment to a core value like excellence. A team dedicated to achieving excellence in everything it does will naturally reach its more specific goals, too, such as greater customer satisfaction, increased sales, enhanced innovation and more productivity—and that's good for the bottom line.

SYNERGY STARTERS: TOTAL COMMITMENT

- Have a brainstorming session at your next meeting about all of the possible client objections and challenges that you might encounter along the way to your goal, and have a positive, open discussion about how you can prepare to deal with them. Take notes and distribute the ideas to the team after the meeting, including contact information for people who have a specific talent in dealing with the different issues based on their background and resources. These people will be your team's lifelines.

- Have each of your teammates jot down a quick PPN report and send it to you and the rest of the team by five o'clock every Friday afternoon. This will bond the teammates, allow them to share ideas and let you know what they've accomplished, where they're focusing their efforts (in case they need to be redirected) and what they think they need in order to be successful.

- Ask your team members why they are here. What are they getting from this job? What do they hope to get from it? What are they not getting that they wish there was more of? I think you'll be pretty surprised by the answers. This exercise will also give you a road map to motivate and inspire the team. This isn't rocket science. Great leaders provide the tools and set the stage for their teammates to motivate and inspire themselves. Why not save some time and ask point-blank what will work for them instead of implementing the trial-and-error method of motivation?

- In small groups, ask your team members to visualize how winning (however that is framed) will look and feel for them personally, not how they think it will affect the organization. (They do care about that a little, just not as much.) Have them think through to the completion of the goal, how great that will feel, what the victory party and incentive trip will be like, and what they will buy with their bonus money. You can even make a fun game out of it and have everyone write on a piece of paper what they would buy with their bonus money, shuffle the papers and pull them out one by one to have everyone guess which teammate has that dream. Winning must be a need for them, not a want. Make them need the feeling and the results of winning, and the motivation to achieve it will be exponentially stronger.

ELEMENT 2:

EMPATHY AND AWARENESS

"A great adventure racing team
operates on four brains, eight legs, eight arms . . .
and one heart."

—**World Class Teams's Motto**

How does it make you feel when you go in to work or go home at the end of the day, and there's a person there who looks directly into your eyes and says, "How are you doing?" You can tell that they genuinely care, and it makes such a difference. Contrast that with coming through the door and hearing, "Okay, here's what you've got to do today. . . . Here's what's going on. . . . I need this done by three o'clock. . . ." There's a disconnection there, and it makes people feel uncomfortable and invisible. Having empathy and awareness for one another is an essential element for creating teams that work.

My Team Merrell/Zanfel Adventure teammates and I were running the Adventure Racing World Championship race in Sweden. We were traversing watery glaciers, so I was wearing waterproof shoes, which are fantastic if you're trying to keep the wet stuff out. But once my feet were submerged and the water got into the shoes from the top, it couldn't get out. So I was essentially walking around in a bathtub for a couple of days, and I developed a nasty case of trench foot. With trench foot, your feet no longer repel moisture. Water gets in between the layers of your skin where all the nerves are. Every time you take a step, the water ticks off those nerve endings, and it feels like an electroshock treatment. For the last few days of the race, I felt like I was walking on pieces of broken glass.

I tried to hang in there and make my way through the race using trekking poles, but every step was agony. I could tell that my teammates wanted me to go faster, but they knew that yelling at someone was not the way to make that happen. They were all pretty cool about it, but one teammate in particular, Ian Edmond, was my salvation. Every time I fell behind, Ian would come back and hold my hand. Sometimes he'd just walk silently alongside me, but other times he'd say, "Okay, Alanis Morissette's *Jagged Little Pill* album," and all of a sudden we'd break into song. Ian and I discovered early in our racing career that we both have brains that capture music and lyrics easily, and we knew a lot of the same tunes. There were a couple of albums that we knew every single word of, and as I lurched along over the glaciers of Sweden, we sang those songs. I don't know if it helped me go any faster, but Ian knew that it would be better for me if he took my brain off the pain. He knew I was suffering, and he took it on himself to be a friend and help me suffer less. And that, in turn, helped our team reach its goal.

The teams that fall apart are the ones that leave the suffering wildebeests alone at the back of the pack and just go on without them, thinking that will make the lame ones go faster. Those teams form little cliques of faster people who end up ignoring or tolerating the slower people. That's not the way a world-class team operates. Winning teams—the ones comprised of folks who have achieved human synergy—stick together no matter what. They start, run and finish the race as a team. They embrace whatever the weaknesses are at that moment and try to make life a little better for the ones who are falling behind.

"PEOPLE WILL ALWAYS REMEMBER HOW YOU TREATED THEM IN THEIR LOWEST MOMENTS."

When you summon your most human side and try to ease the burden of the people around you, it not only bonds your team and gets you to the finish line faster but also helps you become a better person and create a memory with that person. People will always remember how you treated them in their lowest moments. Always. The best teammates are forever aware of that.

HAVE DOUBLE VISION

We spend most of our days in the land of "the way I see it." How can we not? We live behind our own two eyeballs and with our own experiences and backgrounds as our guide. But the most well-connected, successful people understand that in order to bond with and motivate others, you must be able to show them that you truly understand their position, fears, emotions, motivations and drivers before they will give you the permission to help them move to a new way of thinking. It's the key to admission into their world. Without it, you're sunk.

The best team leaders are constantly walking a mile in their teammates' shoes, trying to see, feel and experience their perspectives as a means to a deeper connection and, most important, trust. When you trust, you allow yourself to be motivated and inspired by that person. When you don't feel that your teammates are making an effort to have that double vision—to see things from your perspective as well as their own—and it seems as if they only care about you to the extent that they need you to get across that finish line to achieve their personal goals, your synergy is doomed.

We had been mountain biking, running and paddling for four nonstop days through the sauna-like, leech-infested, soul-destroying jungle of Borneo in the 2000 Eco-Challenge in an effort to build a solid lead on the French Team Intersport. At the end of a fourteen-mile run with all of our paddling gear strapped to our bodies, we raced into a transition area where we were supposed to get a new set of maps and jump into native canoes for an all-night paddle to the Madai Caves. The only downside about a new set of maps is the amount of work it takes a sleep-deprived brain to chart a course, bleary eyed yet demanding of enough precision to find our way across an open ocean to a tiny beach forty miles away. With high winds, strong currents and rolling seas, it was going to be like finding a sandy needle in a haystack.

We were trying to rush our navigator, Ian, through this painstaking process to avoid being sitting ducks when the French ran in. The minutes seemed like hours as we watched and fed Ian, and peered down the trail from which we had just come, certain we would see the headlamps of the French team rounding the turn into the camp at any moment. If they caught up, they could skip doing their maps because they would know we had done ours and could follow right on our tail.

It was an insane pressure cooker for all of us. If Ian didn't complete the maps to his standards, we could be lost at sea all night or worse. If he took too much time to complete them, the French would follow us. There was only a tiny window of time to get out of there, and we just had to preserve our lead. While Ian finished the maps, the rest of us prepared the boat, got our food resupplied, ate and did whatever we could to stay productive. It wasn't long before we had everything ready to go and were all sitting in the boat waiting for Ian so we could paddle away. We stared down the trail, knowing this was the make-or-break moment of the race, and tried to stay calm.

But after over an hour of waiting, our patience ran out. We were desperate to get out of there. I thought, *This is unacceptable! How long can those freaking maps take?* I jogged over to Ian and let loose on him.

"Ian, we've got to go!" I exclaimed. "We've got to get in the boat. We're running out of time. This is taking way too long, dude. We're all so frustrated!"

Poor Ian, the best of the best map gurus who had been working so hard on the course and doing his absolute best to be quick about it, would have been completely justified in blowing up at me. He could have said, "Are you kidding me? I've been working my butt off, and now here you come to me with, *'We're frustrated!'* You guys have eaten a full meal! You've probably even taken a little nap! In the meantime, my brain is about to explode." My anger was gone just like that. He took all the air out of me. Instead of continuing to be openly frustrated with him, I found myself asking him if there was anything else we could do to help.

What if we could be more like that in our everyday lives? We tend to escalate when we could just as easily diffuse. If we let other people see that we're aware, that we understand, that we can put ourselves in their shoes for a moment, we could probably avoid ninety percent of our interpersonal struggles. It doesn't take much. You just have to keep your ego out of the fray and remember that these are the people you are going to take to the finish line with you. Grace or grapple? It's your choice.

By choosing to develop double vision, we inspire our teammates and create an unbreakable bond with them, just as one of my racing buddies did with me during one of our best races, the 2000 Raid Gauloises in Tibet. We were leading the race when we had to complete a canyoning section down a cascade of fifteen waterfalls. The challenge was to rappel down one and land near the top of the next, then rappel down that one and go on to the next, and so on. On several of the rappels, someone's rope ran out, forcing that person to jump into an icy pool wearing a heavy pack and swim out to find a way to the next waterfall.

This particular canyoning exercise was a frustrating, scary experience for me. My teammates were spooked by a team coming up behind us and were in such a rush to get away from the competition that they didn't realize that they had left me behind. When I discovered that I was alone, I started to freak out a little. Not only did I not know where I was, I knew that nobody else knew where I was either. I was cold and alone in the middle of Tibet, and I had no idea where the hell I was going because the course between each waterfall wasn't marked.

I was in tears by the time I got to the tenth or eleventh waterfall and hadn't seen any of my teammates in over an hour. I rappelled down the face of the fall, and when the rope ran out, I dropped reluctantly into the frigid pool below. My waterlogged pack weighed me down. I kicked and flailed, desperately fighting to make it back to the surface and the edge of the pool. I was almost at the end of my rope.

But just as I broke the surface, I saw a hand reaching out for me right in front of my face. I didn't know whose hand it was, and I didn't care. It was my lifeline, so I grabbed it and held on with all my remaining strength. I felt myself being dragged to the edge of the pool and pulled from the water like a rag doll.

And there, standing above me, was my teammate John Howard. Somehow he had realized that I was not with the team anymore, and he had stopped and waited for me. I'll never understand how he knew it, since our team had gone into "every man for himself" mode, but that's the kind of awareness he has. He knew on a visceral level that I was suffering. John had faith that I could make it on my own, but he didn't want me to have to. Instead of trying to prove how great he was, instead of trying to remain at the front of the pack, he knew it was more important for the spirit of the team that nobody was lost or left behind. Believe me, you will always remember the person who remembers you.

In business and life, we spend a lot of time and energy trying to prove to the big shots how great we are as a solo player, but I think it's much more

> "BE THE PERSON WITH DOUBLE VISION."

important to prove who you are to your team. Instead of trying to impress your colleagues, focus instead on inspiring them. Trust me, if you do that, you'll achieve both of those goals at the same time. Be the person with double vision. Be the person who comes back and extends a hand. Be the person everyone knows they can count on. That's the kind of person I want to work with, do business with and live with. That's the kind of person I'll choose for my team every time.

CONNECT TO THE PERSON BEFORE THE POINT

Any salesperson or manager worth their salt can rattle off a list of their product's or service's features and benefits. But the most consistently high-achieving performers understand that developing a platform of trust, human connection and openness with a client is the key to any effective and productive communication. By that I mean the kind of communication or meeting that you don't just walk away from saying, "Well, I gave a great presentation. I hope they go with us." I'm talking about the kind of communication or meeting that you walk away from with a real understanding of why they like your product or service, why they have used your competitor's products for so long or what it's really going to take to get their business. How great would that kind of trust and connection with a client be? And how useful is that kind of information? In essence, you walk away with the blueprint for your future success.

The most experienced teammates (that's what you are during any kind of client interaction) know that you must connect to the person before the point. In order to build the trust that will open the client's mind and heart to you, there must come a moment in which they know that you care about them as a person and not just as a sale. If people like you and trust you, they will want to give you their business, and they will tell you exactly what you have to do to get it. Conversely, if you haven't created that necessary bond up front, whether it's something as small as mentioning that you like their watch, commenting on their office photos from their safari, or noticing an award their company has won and congratulating them on it, your product or service—no matter how great it is—will never see the light of day. This isn't rocket science; it's humanness.

This is the one thing we all have in common: the desire to be seen, understood and interesting to other people. We were born with this desire and ability to bond, and it's amazing to me how often we brush that aside for the sake of being the "professional business person" we think we are all supposed to be. Since when did it become unprofessional to be human?

From when I was in sales, I can't even begin to tell you how many presentations they made us perform on video, to nobody, in

> **"CONNECT TO THE PERSON BEFORE THE POINT."**

which we robotically pointed to the features and benefits on the brochure, practiced holding the pen just so, rehearsed asking the tough challenge questions at the penultimate moment, and other similar exercises. Oh, how victorious we would be!

Hey, it was a good start. It was excellent training. I'm not knocking it. I appreciated their investment in us. But I'll tell you about when I started climbing into the top ranks of the sales force and how I ended up being named rookie of the year at that Fortune 500 pharmaceutical company. I realized that the doctors I was calling on were completely bored with my coming in and talking about the same old product over and over, month in and month out. So one day I decided to take some photos from my latest triathlon to my sales calls and share them with the doctors. *What the heck,* I thought, *at least I wouldn't be bored today.* And when I did that, something changed. When I revealed a little bit about the real me outside of the brochure and the pen and the features and benefits, the doctors shared their own adventures. They told me about their kid who ran track in high school and their wife's dream of running her first sprint triathlon after their first child was born in April and on and on. They lit up. They came alive. I learned more about these surgeons in a few days than I had learned about them in nearly a year. Suddenly I became a real person to them, too, not just a suit with a bag of drugs that they needed to prescribe.

I was successful at sales because I discovered that sometimes the best way to make a sale is to make a friend first. The doctors looked forward to seeing me, and I looked forward to seeing them. We talked about golf, cycling, adventures, kids, dreams, and for just a few minutes, they took a break from being a guy or gal in a white coat to revisit their inner athlete/adventurer or to lecture me in a parental way about how I was going to ruin my joints. And just as they were about to enter that next patient room, the joke with many of them became, "Now, which drug am I supposed to write for again?" And I'd tell them, and they would. The sales part of the sale usually ended up being thirty seconds or less, one thing to remember or one quick point about our product that was discovered in recent research. Even though I was selling a commodity that had several nearly identical competitors, my market share went up. And up. Because my customers were my friends.

I realize that things have changed over the years and that a lot of client interactions aren't that simple. But one thing will always remain the same: the human need to be seen, heard and understood. It may sound weird, but I believe that we have to fall in love with our clients and customers a little bit. Not in a creepy, stalker way, but in a way that subtly lets them know that you care about them, that you have their back, that they can count on you to have their best interests right up there with your own. As a firefighter, I fall in love every single day with the patients we call on. In that moment when I'm taking care of them, I love them. It's momentary and fleeting, but it's real. It's a very cool thing that I wouldn't trade for the world. Of course, it makes me cry a lot because after we take them to the hospital, I often never know what became of them or how they fared. But I cherish that connection with them for the time we have it, and it helps both of us.

I was once called to a medical emergency for a beautiful eighty-year-old woman named Marguerite, whom I will probably never forget. I recognized immediately that she was from New York, like me, and we formed an instant connection. She was having heart trouble and was afraid. While the paramedics got straight to the business of IVs and machines and diagnosis, I was allowed the enviable position of patient care, my favorite spot, because I was the EMT. I reached out and held her hand, and I talked to her about home and her cat and her family while the machines pinged and pads were applied to her chest to check her heart rhythm. After we put her into the back of the ambulance, I climbed in and rode with her all the way to the hospital, holding her hand, touching her hair and telling her that she was going to be okay. She squeezed my hand to let me know that she was still with me, despite going into a quiet place in her mind where she could escape the chest pain. When we wheeled her into the emergency room and I had to release her hand, she turned to me, looked into my eyes with this beautiful angelic expression and said, "I love you." Without hesitation, I said, "I love you, too." I meant it with all my heart. Then I leaned over and kissed her head as the tears streamed down my face. I know I will probably never see her again, as is the case with most of our patients, but she will always have a special place in my heart as someone I loved.

The power of the human connection is sometimes boundless, heartbreakingly beautiful and beyond measure. It can last for a moment or a lifetime. I admit that this is way off the beaten path for a business book, but hey, it's my book, right? I truly believe that what we give in business and life is equally important, if not more important, than what we get. If you set out to give, to love, you will always get that back exponentially in business and in life. So revel in your humanness.

"WHAT YOU GIVE IS AS IMPORTANT AS WHAT YOU GET."

Don't be shy. Reach out to people. Don't hide behind your brochures and your benefits. Be you. If you are the light for other people, meaning that you are their means of feeling good about themselves and of feeling inspired, intelligent, valued (and not feeling sold to), they will respond. Connect to the person. There's something life-affirming and awe-inspiring about being in love for a minute or two. In my opinion, that's the creamy middle in the Oreo of life.

One of the best examples of connecting to the person that I have ever witnessed came during the Eco-Challenge Fiji in 2002. Almost everyone in that race, including all four members of my team, contracted giardiasis, an infection of the small intestine. Giardiasis is caused by contact with water that is contaminated with a microscopic parasite. It triggers diarrhea, gas, bloating, vomiting, fever, fatigue and dehydration—not good symptoms to have when you're trying to run through a sweltering jungle with three other people who also have the same potentially race- and career-ending affliction. For five days, the parasites forced each of us to expel everything in our bodies every fifteen minutes, and from both ends. It was disgusting and horrifying. Our invincible teammate Mike Trisler, a former army Ranger and winner of the prestigious Best Ranger competition, had it worst of all, but there was no way any of us were going to give up.

We had been running for several days when it came time for a paddling leg. The race organizers gave each of the four of us an inflatable kayak and set a dark zone time of six o'clock in the evening, meaning we had to make it to the next transition area and be off the water by then, or pull out of the river onto the bank and stop racing for the night. We plunged into the class II river determined to beat the deadline, but fever and exhaustion had totally wiped out poor Mike. He was laying in his boat, feebly dipping the paddle in and out of the water on each side of the kayak with the hope that he was moving some water and doing something productive. He wasn't. One minute he was asleep, and the next minute he was awake. One minute he was going nowhere, and the next minute he was going in circles. He had no control over his body whatsoever, so we hooked his boat to one of ours with a towline, and off we went through the rapids. By three hours in, Mike had filled up his boat with diarrhea. Yep. While I apologize profusely to you, my new friends, for mentioning poop in my book, every runner out there knows this subject is not only fair game but also a matter of general consultation among training partners. But I digress.

The diarrhea was five inches deep, and Mike had to lay in it for four more hours while we dragged him down that river. He didn't even have the strength to lift his head. Everything, his body and his pack, was becoming covered in filth.

Four o'clock passed, and we kept paddling. Five o'clock came and went, and we were getting desperate. We yelled, "Come on, Mike! Come on, buddy! Keep going!" but the best he could do was flail his paddle around in the air like an orchestra conductor having a bad dream. Bless his heart for trying.

Finally, with only five minutes to spare before the cutoff time, we saw the checkpoint up ahead. We were going to make it. Woo-hoo! The organizers signaled that we had beaten the dark zone by a mere two minutes and could continue the race, a hiking segment. We took our boats out on the opposite side of the river—that is, all except for Mike. He was still floating with the current, too exhausted to move. Our other two teammates suddenly had to "go check the maps," leaving me to take care of the brown mound of Trisler, who was covered in waste from head to toe. It was hideous. I rolled him out of his crap-filled boat. He couldn't stand up, so I laid him on the surface of the river and tried in vain to wash the filth from his body and his pack. *There is no way this guy is going to be able to continue,* I thought. *The next checkpoint is a twelve-mile trek through the jungle. He is so sick, so weak. There is just no way.*

I hoisted Mike's arm and his pack over my shoulder and started trudging across the river. I was stumbling under his weight, fighting to keep my footing on the slippery river bottom, when suddenly I saw a large man break away from the pack of spectators on the opposite bank. He plunged into the water and started making his way toward Mike and me. When he reached us, he grabbed Mike's limp, reeking body, picked him up and began carrying him across the river.

"Come with me," he said over his shoulder. "Come to my house. My wife will feed you, and I'll clean your things."

By now I had been rejoined by my teammates, and we looked at one another in disbelief. We followed the man—this big, beautiful gift from God—as he carried our waterlogged, stinky, feces-covered teammate with the same tenderness and compassion that one would give to a child. He was well over six feet tall, and his skin was the color of dark chocolate. It turns out that he was a local villager who had come to the river out of curiosity to watch the spectacle of a bunch of silly foreigners trying to make their way across the most remote parts of his island. Instead of being amused by our struggle, he was compelled to help.

We followed the man up a hill and arrived at his tiny home. It was a thatched hut of two rooms with a dirt floor. There was a bed behind a curtain in one corner for the man and his wife; their children slept on the floor in front of the fire. Our savior and his wife undressed Mike behind the hut, poured water over him, put him into their one and only bed, and covered him up with the only blankets they owned. They gave us every towel and bit of bedding they had (it wasn't much) and had us strip down to our shorts. The man took all of our filthy clothes back down to the river for a good washing while his wife cooked rice for us. They lit a fire for us and gave us their children's pallets to sleep on.

We stayed with them for four hours. It was the most beautiful thing I have ever experienced. It made all the difference for our team to have these guardian angels come from heaven to feed us, wash our clothes and let us sleep in their little home. But that wasn't all. Later that night, when Mike was feeling strong enough to walk and it was time for us to go, the man led us the twelve miles down the back trail in his bare feet to the village where the next checkpoint was. He handed us off to one of his friends who would look after us from there. Then he turned around and disappeared, and we never saw him again.

That man and his wife wanted nothing from us. They only wanted to take care of us and show us the Fijian spirit and send us on our way. A lot of teams fell apart near the end of that race, but not us. We made it all the way to the finish line in fourth place, fueled by the kindness of that man and his wife. The memory of what they did brings tears to my eyes every time I think about it. I am still in awe of the selflessness, the grace and the beauty of those people who had nothing, standing before complete (and disgusting) strangers, willing to give us everything. In my experience, the human connection is the strongest motivator on Earth.

When things aren't going your way and the rewards that you hoped for at the starting line are no longer important or relevant, it's that human kindness and empathy that we show to one another that can keep you in the game. That man and his wife in Fiji saved our race and, quite possibly, Mike's life by connecting with him and us on such a deep level that it went far beyond any unselfish act or kindness I've ever seen or experienced in my life. I will never forget them, and I will forever be inspired by their gift of showing us the heights to which the human spirit can elevate a team.

FOCUS ON COACHING VERSUS CRITICISM

If you are mentally pointing a finger at someone when you discuss things that need to be changed (*you* need more training, *you* blew that sale, *you* were unprepared and so on), your teammate is going to instantly put up a wall and get defensive. But if you mentally extend a hand instead (here's what I'm seeing, share your challenges with me, how can I help? what do you need from us to be successful?), then there is a much greater chance that your message will be received in good faith and that positive change will be made. It's easy to criticize. It's much harder and much more worthwhile to coach instead, to offer a towline that lets your teammates know you believe in them. Consciously think about extending a hand to your teammates when behaviors need to change instead of pointing a finger. You will be closer to your goal and be a more well-respected leader at the same time.

UNDERSTAND THAT WE WORK FOR PEOPLE, NOT FOR COMPANIES

We all start out just working for a company, but somewhere along the line we end up working for the people around us, for our leaders, our teammates. The people around you are your reason for getting up in the morning, the means to feeling good about yourself, the folks you want to inspire, laugh with, kibitz with and be inspired by. We've all had the experience of staying with a particular company way too long because we were so tied in with a fantastic leader or a great team. Conversely, people flee from great companies with huge opportunities for advancement because they'd rather chew their own arm off than spend one more day with the circus that is their leadership or their team.

Building a high-performance organization starts with who you are every day for your team. You set the vibe, you set the stage for how people are treated and you ensure that the people around you are valued, trusted and inspired. Every day you have to go into work being the person that your teammates hope you are, that they want you to be, that they trust to make good decisions and that they are motivated by. At the end of the day, they will work for you and for each other, not just for the company. The wise team leader always remembers that.

"BUILDING A HIGH-PERFORMANCE ORGANIZATION STARTS WITH WHO YOU ARE EVERY DAY FOR YOUR TEAM."

It was late October of 2007, and a wave of crazy, wind-driven wildfires was barreling through San Diego County. At 4:30 a.m. on October 23, our fire station got the call to respond to the Rancho Bernardo suburb, where the advancing blazes had suddenly picked up speed and were threatening hundreds of homes. On the ride in, we listened to harrowing reports of people being trapped in their swimming pools and on the upper levels of their houses.

We were one of the first-strike crews to arrive on the scene, and what we found was our worst nightmare. The embers and flames were jumping from house to house, creating a patchwork of fire for blocks around. It looked like hell on Earth. Each captain decided to focus on a one-block area, so we kept driving until we found a street that no other crew was on. As we bailed out of our engine, our overwhelmed chief's last words to us were, "Just do what you can." I felt so small and insignificant and scared.

My crew and I established a triage system as we moved from house to house. Some were already too far gone, and we had to let them go and move on to the next one, focusing only on protecting those that were not yet engulfed. I saw one that was just beginning to catch fire up in the eaves, and I thought we might be able to save it. As I dragged my hose across the lawn, I heard something crunching under my feet. In the predawn light, I could see that I was standing on top of a pile of framed pictures that were scattered over the grass. *The people who live here probably ran down the hall grabbing whatever they could on their way out the door, hoping to save it from the fire,* I thought. There were pictures of a little girl wearing a tutu and ballet shoes, a boy playing soccer, a chubby baby, a proud mom and dad surrounded by their smiling children.

In that fleeting instant, something clicked in my brain—and in my heart. This was not just some random house in Rancho Bernardo anymore. It was this family's home. And I was no longer working for the San Diego Fire Department. I was working for this family.

Suddenly I didn't feel small or insignificant or scared anymore. I was alive and inspired. We had to do whatever it took to save this house. I called my crew over, and we started battling the fire in the eaves before it could take hold, hosing everything down, moving stuff out of the way. There was a little soccer net and a dollhouse in the backyard, and I remember thinking that "Billy" and "Susie" were definitely going to want those, so we pulled them across the street before they got trampled or burned. That family unknowingly reached out to me and my crew and connected with us on a human level, and we tried so much harder because of it. And we saved their home.

We went back to the neighborhood the next day, after everything had calmed down and the fire had moved on. When we pulled up in front of that residence, the family was standing on their lawn holding hands and looking up at their home. The mother was crying with gratitude. It was such a great moment for all of us because we actually got to complete that circle of connection with those people.

I know we sometimes feel funny about letting people "see" us and telling them things about our lives, but trust me, people want to know you. They want to feel closer to you. It is a beautiful thing when people want to work for you as a person and not for the title on your business card. The human connection is the strongest motivator on Earth. Why wouldn't we use it to create bonds and motivate our teammates in our businesses, too?

EMPATHY AND AWARENESS: A BUSINESS CASE STUDY

In February 2011, *Fortune* magazine released its annual list of the "100 Best Companies to Work For." For the second year, the number one company on that list was SAS, a North Carolina software firm. SAS provides on-site health care, day care and summer camps for its employees' kids, a gym, a beauty salon, car cleaning services, job sharing, telecommuting and an array of other perks that most workers can only dream of. One SAS manager said, "People stay at SAS in large part because they are happy, but to dig a little deeper, I would argue that people don't leave SAS because they feel regarded—seen, attended to and cared for. I have stayed for that reason, and love what I do for that reason."[2]

He's not alone: SAS reported a voluntary turnover rate of only two percent, with over 45,000 applicants vying for 151 available jobs. The company's revenue in 2009 was $2.3 billion.

It looks as if that touchy-feely stuff is working out pretty well for SAS. It will pay dividends for your team, too.

SYNERGY STARTERS: EMPATHY AND AWARENESS

A fun synergy starter for your team (and also a great party starter, by the way) is to have each person fill out a life pyramid consisting of three goals they have in life, two things people would be surprised to know about them and one peak experience. I've included mine as an example. Talk about how you can help one another achieve the goals.

---

2   "100 Best Companies to Work For," *Fortune,* February 7, 2011, http://money.cnn.com/ magazines/fortune/bestcompanies/2011/snapshots/1.html (accessed April 6, 2011).

One peak experience

**SEEING
MY NEPHEW'S
BIRTH**

Two things people
would be surprised
to know about you

I CAN RIDE A UNICYCLE

I WAS A NATIONAL JUDO CHAMPION

Three
life goals

TO BE THE PERSON THAT DOGS THINK I AM

**TO HELP OVER 1000 ATHENAS
EACH YEAR LIVE AN ADVENTUROUS DREAM**

**TO DEVELOP *PROJECT ATHENA ADVENTURE TRAVEL* TO
HELP EVERYONE LIVE ADVENTUROUS DREAMS WHILE RAISING
MONEY FOR THE PROJECT ATHENA FOUNDATION**

ELEMENT 3:

ADVERSITY MANAGEMENT

"Change is the only thing that stays the same. It is our response to that change that dictates our success."

—Chief Alan Brunacini, Phoenix Fire Department

All of us know that no matter how much we try, no matter how much we plan, no matter how much we know, no matter how much we prepare, sometimes the journey ends very badly. You've probably seen that anti-Successories poster of the trout, which had probably been swimming upstream for weeks to get to its spawning area, jumping out of the water right into the mouth of a bear that was lucky enough to wade into the river at just the right spot. The caption reads, "The journey of a thousand miles sometimes ends very, very badly." Everyone knows that some days we're the bear and everything is going our way, the fish are jumping out of the stream straight into our mouths, and some days we're the trout. So how do great team builders continue to inspire their teams on those trout days? In other words, how do high-performance teams handle the tough times, react to changes and roll with the punches in a way that allows them to be consistently successful, year in and year out? The most important thing is to start with the right mind-set and attitude.

SEE CHALLENGES VERSUS ROADBLOCKS

Their attitude was the main reason I preferred racing with the Australians and the New Zealanders. My Aussie friends always say, "No worries, mate!" And regardless of what was going wrong, my New Zealand teammates' favorite expression was, "Aw, she'll be 'roiiit." You could be telling them, "Mate, your leg's half off!" and the response would be, "Aw yeeeah, she'll be 'roiiit, just a flesh wound." Every day was like a Monty Python movie with these guys. With my favorite teammates, a ten-day race across the most remote places on Earth with the circumstances changing minute to minute was always an interesting and challenging journey, a long series of problems to tackle and obstacles to overcome together. With the wrong teammates, everything is a deal breaker, a race-ending catastrophe, and brainstorming comes to a standstill. I loved the Kiwi and Aussie way because nothing was ever a lost cause in their minds. It was always going to be okay somehow. Whether they were faking their way through that degree of confidence was irrelevant because confidence begets hope, and hope is what keeps us mentally in the game to brainstorm solutions. When someone tells you, "Hey, we have a challenge here!" there's a feeling of rising to the occasion, a feeling that what lies ahead is just another opportunity to prove ourselves.

Conversely, when a teammate gives up hope and says, "It's over. There's no way out for us," brainstorming is shut down, and entropy takes over our souls. That's not to say that we shouldn't master the tactical agility to make a U-turn whenever necessary, because that's an important skill. But the best teambuilders can even position a U-turn in a positive light, as merely a new set of challenges.

The only time my buddy Neil Jones ever admitted that we had a roadblock versus a challenge was in the middle of the 2001 Adventure Racing World Championships in New Zealand. Jonesy and I were paddling together in a double kayak toward a checkpoint set up on a windswept beach. There were huge swells and a storm surge for the entire six-hour paddle, and as we approached the finish line, the waves became six-feet-overhead crushers that were eating up teams and spitting them out. I'm not a big fan of wave riding to start with, especially when we're in an easily breakable carbon fiber kayak with all of our mandatory race gear on the deck and in the hull. I was petrified. As we neared the beach, we saw what looked like a yard sale: backpacks, paddles and dry bags were scattered on the surface of the water in every direction, and several riderless boats, many in pieces, bobbed happily along the surf line.

I need a lot of reassurance when I'm nervous, so in the last few minutes of our approach to the beach, I kept yelling back to Jonesy, "Are we okay?"

"Aw yeeeah, mate, we're 'roiiit! Keep paddlin'," he shouted.

Whew! What a relief that Jonesy thinks we're all right, I thought as I dug in and paddled even harder. This sequence of questioning and reassurance went back and forth several times over the next couple of minutes, with Jonesy patiently responding, "Aw, we're perfect, mate! This is just like the conditions in New Zealand. Easy day!"

Then my worst fear was realized. A few seconds later, a six-foot wave came up directly underneath our kayak. As Jonesy

> **"FOR MAXIMUM PERFORMANCE, HOPE IS A BETTER PLACE THAN FEAR."**

vaulted over the top of my head, he looked down and yelled, "Aw, mate, we're *stuffed!*"

It wasn't until Jonesy was absolutely certain we were stuffed that he felt compelled to let me know, which allowed me to keep on paddling with hope versus fear. Hope is a much better place than fear to operate from for maximum performance. Reassuring and encouraging us to keep going even though the waves are crashing all around us—that's what world-class team builders do.

THE HOPE OF SUCCESS VERSUS THE FEAR OF FAILURE

When we are faced with a challenge, whether it's in sports, academics, business or relationships, many of us operate out of a fear of failure. We focus our attention and efforts on not falling short, on trying to stay just one step ahead. But the greatest team builders think differently. Sure, they are cognizant of the possibility of failure, and they prepare to deal with the things that go sideways, but their main focus is on doing what it takes to *win* versus simply *not lose*. There is a subtle yet profound distinction between the two.

Ian Adamson showed me this success-focused mind-set in a race back in 1998. It was day seven of a nine-day race across the mountains and jungles of Ecuador, and we were running neck and neck with the French. We had a twenty-four-hour lead on the rest of the field, but we and the French were locked in this death race to the finish. Our team jumped into our boats for a whitewater rafting section, with the French team right behind us. As we were paddling along trying to put distance between us and them, I, being a "fear of failure" person at the time, kept looking back to see where they were, to see if they were gaining on us, to see if they were falling back. After a while, Ian, who was behind me and guiding our boat, became totally annoyed by where my focus was. After about the thirtieth time I turned around, he started putting his hand up and blocking my vision. After about the sixtieth time I turned around, he was so mad about where my focus was that he threw his paddle down in the boat (now nobody's steering!) and grabbed the top of my head, spun it back around to face forward and growled in my ear, "Winning is *that* way."

Honestly, I have to say that Ian's little pep talk means a lot more to me now than it did then. I spent the next hour trying to decide on a good way to dispose of his body, perhaps by strapping it to the heaviest bag in our boat and making some nice cement shoes.

But my teammate on the other side of the boat, Steve Gurney, heard Ian's comment, and luckily it inspired far less sinister and ultimately more useful thoughts. Prompted by a sudden and renewed focus on what it would really take to win, he began mulling over the available tools he could use to put some serious distance between us and the French. Staying just one step ahead of them was too close for comfort. Because Steve was so focused on success and not consumed by the fear of failure, he came up with something truly amazing.

At the next transition, during which we switched from one whitewater raft to two separate inflatable canoes per team, he told us that he had an idea and asked us to trust him. As the French quickly switched into their two canoes and launched back into the river, leaving us behind on the shore, we anxiously awaited the unveiling of

Steve's master plan. This was really risky. The French were gone and paddling away from us toward the finish line, putting greater distance between us minute by minute. Tick, tick, tick, tick.

"Get out our climbing rope," Steve said as he motioned to one of the gear boxes, "and grab the kayak paddles."

Kayak paddles? These were canoes. The French had now been gone fifteen minutes, but Steve was concentrating too hard on winning to be bothered by that. He took our climbing rope and began tying our two inflatable canoes together through all of the steel rings along the outside flanks of each boat. The guys, finally getting a feel for his plan, jumped in to help. I put our kayak paddles together and watched the clock. Twenty minutes . . . twenty-five . . . thirty. Were we sitting ducks or brilliant masterminds? Only time would tell.

Forty minutes later, we were back on the water, and the chase was on. But now we were all paddling, in essence, in one boat and with the power of kayak paddles with blades on both sides instead of one. We were flying! Five kayak blades in perfect synchronicity, grabbing and throwing the water behind us, on a mission to track down the French. It was an incredible feeling, one that I will never forget. It took us three nail-biting hours to catch them, but catch them we did. At first they appeared on the long straightaway as two tiny insects with beating wings. Then they slowly but inevitably morphed into two gray centipedes with multiple moving legs (granted, I was quite sleep-deprived at this point) and finally into a team of French adventure racers, hoping against hope that the sound of splashing water behind them was a figment of their imaginations. The moment when we passed them was one of the most memorable of my racing career. They were so surprised to see us that one of their boats nearly made a complete 360 in the water as they collectively looked over their shoulders to watch the Steve Gurney Missile pass by.

After racing neck and neck with these guys for eight days and calling them The Terminators because they just wouldn't die, we passed them like they were standing still, and we never looked back. We ended up beating them by two hours, and in doing so we became the first North Americans to ever win a major international adventure race.

We carried that "hope of success" attitude right from Ecuador to our next world championship race through the jungles of Borneo at the 2000 Eco-Challenge, and that little shift in thinking created the make-or-break moment of our race: we were either going to win big or almost die trying. Night was falling on day three, and we were hiking a trail alongside a river on our way to the next transition area. On the map, and based on the fact that this was supposed to be a hiking section, the trail appeared to be the only way to get to where we were going. Our predicted hiking pace indicated that this would be at least a five-hour trek to the next transition. We stared down the muddy, rutty, uneven animal track and realized that this might be a far greater challenge than it appeared on paper. We were moving like pond scum, and dark was approaching. The prospect of bushwhacking through dense brush on a treacherous and occasionally nonexistent trail all night long was starting to weigh heavily on our minds and psyches when Ian had a sudden revelation.

"Hey, why don't we jump in the river and let it carry us downstream? The current is running faster than we can go on foot."

We turned to look at the river rushing past us. This wasn't some lazy river ambling by; it was whitewater. To jump in it would be nuts. It would be a death wish in the dark. It would be a major risk.

It was sheer genius.

We knew that most of the teams ahead of and behind us would never even dream of jumping into the river, which made it all the more alluring as a secret weapon. We knew that the other teams would be thinking, *This is the hiking trail we've got to go down. To keep from losing ground, all we have to do is walk a little faster than the teams behind us.* That was a strategy based on fear of failure. Then a "ruled by success" competitor like Ian comes along and thinks completely out of the box. It would indeed be a risk, but sometimes that's what it takes to win versus simply not lose.

> **"BETTER TO LIGHT A CANDLE THAN TO CURSE THE DARKNESS."**
> —Chinese proverb

We discussed the pros and cons of riding the river. At best it would vault us to the lead, and we would emerge at the next transition area like a pack of soaking wet rats, shaking and banged up but victorious. At worst we would lose somebody, and there would be the heartbreak of what-if for years to come. But the reality would probably be somewhere between those two extremes. We decided it was a risk worth taking. These were the make-or-break moments of a racing career, the moments that we would be recounting to our grandkids from a rocking chair one day. Or writing about in a book (hee-hee!). I remember being cognizant of that in the moment and smiling to myself. We were somehow going to make history with this crazy, stunningly silly stunt, and we would emerge as either heroes or the tragic stuff of adventure racing legend.

I admit that making that first leap into the whitewater was scary as hell. We had no life vests, and the river had not been scouted by the race officials for snags, waterfalls, huge rapids or strainers—all things that could kill us in a heartbeat. This was the wilds of the Borneo rain forest, and there had been a deluge of rain about an hour before, which had caused the water levels in the canyon to rise alarmingly. Conditions were changing minute to minute, and not for the best.

It was pitch-black within thirty minutes of our "first descent" (uncharted) whitewater swim, and the only way I could see my team-mates was in the bobbing of their headlamps ahead as they swam for their lives through the rapids just ahead of me. I had never been so afraid and so alone in my life. The guys wouldn't be able to save me, nor I them. For more than two harrowing hours, we swam a continual series of class II and III rapids in the dark, never knowing what was coming next. When we could hear the sound of thundering rapids ahead, we would regroup as much as possible in an eddy or behind a boulder and then go solo into the tumultuous nothingness, bobbing away from the safety of the team and hoping for the best. One by one, the headlamps would disappear around the corner at breakneck speed, and then it would be my turn. All I could think was that my dad was going to kill me if I died!

My heart racing and nauseated from fear, I let go of the safety of the rocks and went back into the rapids every time, even though everything in my body was telling me not to. I had no other choice. The guys were gone. If we were separated now, they might never find me again. As was the case in every adventure race, I was forced into a position that I had come to know and love as bravery by default.

Hey, whether it's actual bravery or bravery by default, the outcome is still the same. I prayed for the safe delivery of my team from this dangerous liquid man (and woman) eater. After what seemed like an eternity, my prayers were answered. The lights of the next village grew brighter and brighter, and one by one we swam with all the energy we had to the nearest eddy and emerged from the water onto the muddy riverbank like exhausted navy SEALs.

The looks on the faces of the race officials were priceless. They weren't expecting teams for a few more hours, and they were expecting them on the other side of the river and on the trail. They most certainly weren't expecting *our* team. And why were we dripping like drowned rats? Word spread like wildfire throughout the transition area, and soon some of the race organizers and members of the media came running across the field, excited to be part of the drama that was unfolding. They couldn't believe it. Neither could we. We had gone from fourth place to the front of the pack, with no other teams in sight!

To our amazement, we finished that section two hours ahead of the race organizers' fastest predicted time for that hiking leg, and we held that lead for the duration of the race. Yes, it was risky. Yes, it wasn't the smartest thing we'd ever done. And yes, it could have turned out very differently. But my teammates are big believers in doing what it takes to win races versus simply not losing them. And therein lies the difference between the world champions and the rest of the field. Teams that operate from a place of safety, security and comfort can undoubtedly make it to the finish line consistently and have an incredibly long and successful career, but more often than not, the podium spots are reserved for the brave, whether by default or otherwise.

One of the most compelling illustrations of this concept comes from the firefighting world, from an incident known as the Mann Gulch fire. With a stunningly courageous move that was ruled by the hope of success, one brave firefighter not only saved his own life but also changed the way we fight brushfires to this day.

It was a hot August afternoon in 1949 when a report came in to the Missoula, Montana, firestation of a small fire in Helena National Forest. Sixteen jumpers—specially trained firefighters who parachute into forest fire zones—were flown to the site. The jumpers were mostly World War II veterans between the ages of seventeen and thirty-three, and their foreman was Wagner "Wag" Dodge. From the air the fire looked manageable. But shortly after the jumpers landed in the gulch, the wind shifted, and the fire jumped from one ridge to another. In a matter of moments, the men were face to face with a raging inferno that was charging up the mountain toward them, fueled by dry brush and intense uphill drafts.

The firefighters tried to scramble up and outrun the twenty-foot wall of flames that was lapping at their backs, but it was treacherous and difficult terrain. The men were no match for the speed of the blaze that relentlessly pursued them, and they were surrounded by dry grass and light, flashy fuels. It was the worst-case scenario for a firefighter. That's when Wag Dodge suddenly stopped, lit a match and set fire to the dry grass at his feet. His crew looked on in shock. They were running from flames, and Dodge was lighting a match? Insanity!

But Dodge had a plan. His idea was to burn off a swath of grass between his men and the fast-approaching fire, leaving the blaze with insufficient fuel to continue its deadly upward advance—in effect, creating a safe blackened zone where his men could survive while the flames naturally gravitated toward the more fuel-dense areas outside of the burn. No one had ever seen that technique done before. The firefighter who was second in command shouted, "To hell with that!" and ran away, followed by the rest of the firefighters—leaving only Dodge, who doused himself with water, covered his face with a damp cloth and lay prone on the ground within the safety zone he had created. As the inferno raged all around him, the rest of his crew ran for their lives against flames that were moving at a rate of ten feet per second. It was a fruitless race. Only Dodge and two other firefighters who ran laterally to a lower ridgeline made it out of Mann Gulch alive that day.

Wag Dodge demonstrated incredible courage in the face of adversity. He shattered the norm and did something that had never been done before in an effort to save his life, while the others were focused on not losing theirs. In all honesty, I can't say that if I were in that position, I wouldn't be running for the top of the mountain myself. I can't even imagine what Wag Dodge felt like, making that split-second decision to choose saving his life versus running from death. But thanks to Dodge and his backfire (as it is now called, a staple tool for fighting brushfires) and the new safety regulations that followed in the wake of the Mann Gulch fire, I hope and pray that I will never have to find out. Every time I'm on the front line of a brushfire and my heart is racing and I'm feeling intense heat lapping at my back and burning my feet, I think of Wag Dodge and his incredible bravery, and I am inspired. And grateful.

When you and your team are faced with a challenge, what is it that guides you? Is it the hope of success or the fear of failure?

Pledge to be led by hope because hope opens doors and expands hearts and minds. The hope of success is often the mother of invention and the catalyst that wins contracts, changes an industry, wins races,

"BE GUIDED BY THE HOPE OF SUCCESS, NOT THE FEAR OF FAILURE."

saves lives. The fear of failure results in a life among the safe, the "good" and the comfortable. When you leave the playing field, what will you be remembered for?

ACCEPT AND EMBRACE ADVERSITY AS A CHANCE TO LEARN AND EXCEL

Great winners not only have hope but also embrace setbacks as a chance to learn and excel. I knew this on an intellectual level after having raced with so many inspiring and inspired teammates, but I was forced to embrace the power of the setback on a personal level in 2007. I hit the deck in the world championships in Scotland that year, meaning I was in so much pain that I took one final step and fell to the ground on the fifth day of the race, the day that my team was climbing the biggest peak in the country, Ben Nevis. My teammates took all of my gear and put me on a towline. During the last thirty-six hours of that race, I often had to physically pick up my leg and move it forward because it would no longer respond to signals from my brain. My body knew that my race was over long before my mind did. Against all odds and through amazing synergy, we crossed the finish line, but in a disappointing sixth place.

I felt terrible about letting my team down on the final day. It was completely out of character for my body to not rise to the occasion during a race. I knew on a gut level that something was terribly wrong. My fiancé, Jeff, had to carry me on and off the plane, and I finally had to admit that this wasn't something I could just work through, as I had done with every other setback in my athletic life. A few days after we arrived home, I saw an orthopedic surgeon. After listening to my symptoms, he took an X-ray and popped it up onto the light box.

"Yep, just as I thought. You have stage four osteoarthritis in both hips," he said, without flourish or preamble. "No more cartilage, just bone on bone now on this side. Your racing career is over. You're never going to run again."

Osteoarthritis? I think my grandmother had that in her knuckles. He could not be talking about me. This wasn't happening. This was just a bad dream, and I was going to wake up at any moment. I felt like I had been punched in the stomach. Waves of nausea crashed over me, and the room started spinning. I was only forty years old—the prime of my life as an endurance racer. I wasn't ready for this. My adventure racing friends called me the Human Cockroach because I could make it through anything: freezing hail, blazing 130-degree heat, days on end with minimal food, no sleep and little water. I had never had any major physical issues—no knee problems, no race-ending injuries, rarely even a blister. I was the one who moved forward on the course at all costs, never lightning fast, mind you, but never stopping. I was going to be the last woman standing in the nuclear winter! And something like osteoarthritis was going to take me out? No way.

I explained to him that he was wrong about my never running or racing again and that I was positive I could make it through with some good anti-inflammatory meds. He smiled and wrote me a prescription for sixty ibuprofen 800 tablets. I grabbed the prescription and told him I'd see him in two years, to which he replied, "I'll see you in two weeks."

Guess who was right? I'll give you a hint: not me.

I just needed time to wrap my brain around the fact that my body, which had done seven years of elite gymnastics, three years of track, six years of diving, six years of judo, ten Ironman triathlons and thirty-six expedition-length adventure races, had given up the ghost. My crazy Rottweiler of a body, which for years had successfully raced among the little greyhound endurance athletes of the world, had ground to a halt. The Human Cockroach had inadvertently wandered into a roach motel.

It took a few days to finally stop figuratively kicking and screaming and finally accept the truth. I had had forty amazing years of competition and adventures. I might have to switch sports for a while, but this wasn't cancer. This was not a death sentence. This was just a chance to become bionic! I think when I made the conscious decision to put on my beanie cap of gratitude for what I still had (versus mourning what I was losing) and the fact that in the lottery of life's setbacks, this was a winner, it changed everything. Into every life some rain must fall. At least this was the sun-shower of rainstorms. I decided to be ruled by the hope of success and opt for the chance of getting my life back, in the form of Birmingham hip resurfacing. The name of the procedure is a pretty big misnomer. *Resurfacing* sounds kind of nice, like you're having a facial or something. But the truth is that the resurfacing procedure starts with the complete dislocation of one's leg (trust me, do not watch the online video of this surgery) and ends with a new chrome ball and socket, held in place by a charming three-inch spike hammered into the top of one's femur.

I was on crutches and a cane for four weeks, and then I slowly but surely got back to work, back onto my bike, back into a boat and finally back to running. In early 2008, I ran a 155-mile multiday ultramarathon in Vietnam with my team. It hurt, but I was getting my life back. I was going to be okay(ish)!

Then, as if on cue based on my surgeon's predictions, the other shoe dropped. In June of 2009, I hit the deck again in the middle of a race. Only this time my teammates had to carry me that last eight miles to the finish line. The pain was off the charts. I couldn't put an ounce of weight on my leg without the feeling that someone was jamming a knife into my groin. Not again. Why couldn't I have issues with something that we only have one of? I was pushed through the airport in a wheelchair, pulling my bike box and my gear box along with me on either side. I was back in surgery for my second resurfacing ten days later.

Going through the process of getting these bionic hips, I realized how important and how precious it is to be able to

> **"YOU DO WHAT YOU CAN FOR AS LONG AS YOU CAN, AND WHEN YOU FINALLY CAN'T, YOU DO THE NEXT BEST THING. YOU BACK UP BUT YOU DON'T GIVE UP."**
> —Chuck Yeager

get out and play with my best friends in the most remote and stunning places on Earth, and what that deep connection to our friends and the planet does for our psyches and our soul. I had taken it for granted when I was healthy, and I knew I would never take it for granted again. If I could only run again, if I could only race again, I would embrace and be grateful for every moment, and not just fear failure as I had done for the majority of my prior races.

Right after my first hip resurfacing, I started planning adventures in my head and putting together a roster of the people with whom I would like to share these adventures. At the top of the list were my two best girlfriends, Melissa Cleary and Louise Cooper. They had also been through hell as survivors of rheumatoid arthritis and breast cancer, respectively, and they would be right there with me in spirit and in person if sometimes I had to walk instead of run, ride bikes instead of walk or eat chocolate and drink wine instead of any of it. They would understand completely, as they had been through it themselves.

And then it hit me. What about other survivors of medical setbacks who don't have adventures to look forward to? What if they don't have this amazing circle of understanding and likeminded goddesses to help them through their recovery? And so the non-profit Project Athena Foundation was born. I was so grateful to have adventures ahead and awesome ibuprofen-sharing, limping, giggling, suffering, inflamed friends to do them with; I wanted to give that sense of hope and excitement to other women like us to help them with their own recoveries, and to help them see the light at the end of those long tunnels of hopelessness in which they wondered if anything was ever going to be OK again. I chose the name

Project Athena because Athena was the goddess of wisdom and war. My wise friends had proven to me that through war comes wisdom. I was inspired by them, just as I hoped that together, we would inspire others.

Project Athena isn't about being everything you were. It's about making the very best of who you are today, and giving you a sense of belonging, confidence and connection to your new self and the goddesses and gods who've helped you get your groove back. Since 2009, we've been giving out grants to survivors for equipment, airfare, entry fees, coaching and whatever else they need to help them live their adventurous dreams. Dreams that range from running on the Great Wall of China to crossing the finish line in a local 5K, and it's the most rewarding thing I have ever done in my life. I am certain that Melissa and Louise, Project Athena's Angel of Hope and Chief Inspiration Officer, would agree with me.

Eventually, we hope to extend our reach to hundreds of survivors each year, and to that end, we are expanding our Fundraising God/Goddess Adventures (for regular healthy people who want to help us raise funds for our survivors) to include Grand Canyon treks, multisport adventures in the Florida Keys and mountaineering trips. You can find the scoop on our website at www.projectathena.org. Yes, that was a shameless plug for you to come join us.

I guess the moral of the story is that none of this life-changing and life-affirming stuff would have happened had there been more cartilage in the world. Sometimes a little setback is the universe showing us a new way to leap forward.

Along those same lines, we've all heard the old saying, *when the universe closes a door, it opens a window,* right? Well, I half believe that. I like to say instead that when the universe closes a door, you get out a chain saw and carve out a window.

****

After my second hip surgery, I came to grips with the fact that I might not be able to adventure race at a world-class level with two metal-on-metal hips, so I decided instead to focus on what I *could* do, and one of those things was paddling. I knew that the paddling sections of an adventure race were where I felt my strongest and happiest, so it seemed to make sense to try to stick with my strengths, especially if it didn't involve metal parts clanging together. I decided to get into a kayak and try my first big solo race: a 460-mile wilderness paddling adventure from Whitehorse to Dawson City in the Yukon Territory of western Canada. No, I couldn't start with something less ridiculous (I know you're wondering). You know me by now. I'm not smart, just "good pioneer stock," as my old fire captain would say. After forty-three scary, gut-wrenching, beautiful, bone-chilling, soggy, smelly, blistered, chafed, rash-y hours out there alone in the Yukon, tiny and insignificant in the vastness of a heartrending landscape of moving water, sky, rain and eagles, I paddled into the town of Dawson City, spent but thrilled. I had found a new love. I was not just a good pad-dler; I was a very good paddler.

Until that race, I had no idea. For years I had given the credit to whichever teammate was behind me in our double kayak. For years I was convinced that we were at the front of the pack because of my teammate's incredible talent, which was true, but in that paddling race through the Yukon, I discovered that I wasn't just a paperweight in a boat either. To my surprise, when I arrived at the finish line at 1:00 a.m., my Jeff came running down the ramp and told me I finished in third place.

Wow! How cool is that? Third place in my first big race! I asked the name of the girls who were first and second in the women's division.

"Girls? Honey, you were third place solo overall! You are the eighth boat in, including the teams!"

I knew I was hearing things. No way. There were a hundred and ten boats in that race, including thirty solo paddlers—twenty-four of them men. I knew then that everything was going to be okay, that I wouldn't be all that I was, but there was a whole new and exciting world opening up for me in a sport that I may never have tried, and didn't even know existed.

At forty-three years old, I had discovered a completely new talent, like finding out by accident that if I flapped my arms, I could fly but had gone half my life without knowing it. I also knew that I had some very special guardian angels looking out for my spirit, and I thanked them from the bottom of my heart. I would be an athlete again at the top of my game. What a gift, one that I will never, ever take for granted.

****

I think we honor our guardian angels by using the tools they have given us in a worthy pursuit, especially one in which we are able to help or inspire others. I still don't know whether this gift was discovered by accident or I was in some way guided toward my unique strength. At the risk of having this book end up in the mystical section in the library, I'm not afraid to say that I believe when we are following the strongest flow in this river that we call our lives, great things come our way. In fact, that's often how we know we are doing the right things and

"LIFE IS NOT ABOUT WAITING FOR THE STORMS TO PASS. IT'S ABOUT LEARNING TO DANCE IN THE RAIN."
—unknown

following the best path. When we're in the flow, everything is easy and things seem to fall into place. Great jobs, great relationships, happiness, security and love come streaming toward us. When we are out of the good flow, everything is an effort. There are eddies and waves and dangerous boulders, and we can't seem to get where we want to go or receive anything we need.

If you're figuratively fighting the current and feeling like you're constantly trying to swim upstream in your life, look around and find the flow. Live in your strengths rather than spending time shoring up your weaknesses. Reach out to friends and connect. Find people to help and to love instead of waiting for that love to happen to you. Get healthier, get outside, join a club. That's where you'll find your flow.

After four years of wondering and questioning whether I was going to be an athlete again, I found my flow in the Yukon River. And there was even a rainbow to prove it, which appeared over my shoulder when I started praying for relief from the torrential downpour and the gale-force winds that were throwing my boat all over the river and threatening to tip me over.

****

Now, back to some more adversity management. It couldn't so easily be a happy ending, could it? A few months before this race in the Yukon, my newest hip started hurting again. I went to New York to see the specialist who had performed that surgery, and the news wasn't great. I had a stress fracture in my femoral neck. We're still not exactly sure why, aside from the fact that I may have had a preexisting stress fracture that couldn't be seen on the pre-op X-ray. I was desperately trying to heal it so I wouldn't have to undergo a third major hip surgery in just about as many years, but to no avail. After seven months of paddling and taking it easy on weight-bearing activity (well, aside from being a firefighter and all), my doctor and I came to the conclusion that I would need a third hip surgery, this time a total hip replacement. It was scheduled for November 22, 2010. I had to do something special to live in the flow one more time before I went under the knife—or bone saw, as was the case here.

I wanted to follow in my teammate Carter Johnson's footsteps and try setting a Guinness world record for paddling a kayak the longest distance ever recorded on flat water for a female in a twenty-four-hour period. Why not dream big? So on October 28, 2010, Carter and I set out on Lake Nacimiento in southern California to tackle the men's and women's world records simultaneously on a tightly monitored and surveyed 3.11-mile straight-line course.

"LIVE IN YOUR STRENGTHS RATHER THAN SPENDING TIME SHORING UP YOUR WEAKNESSES."

Because of an impending storm that was due the following evening, we scrambled and rallied immediately upon our arrival and started out in the dark, twelve hours before our planned launch. As I paddled my not-quite-ready self and not-quite-ready gear out to the starting line, I acknowledged that it wasn't pretty, but we weren't going to let the pursuit of perfection hinder our progress. At precisely 7:30 p.m., Jeff and our good pal Addie Goodvibes (yes, that's his real name), who also served as our course monitors, photographers, videographers, chefs, cheerleaders, water bearers and motivators, sounded the air horn to indicate the start of the official twenty-four-hour time clock. Into the abyss we went.

Slowly Carter pulled away from me, and I was alone, paddling on the glassy stillness of the lake, back and forth on the 3.11-mile course. Back and forth. I let my thoughts wander for a while, but eventually I was all out of those. There's only so much that I can store in my noggin. I needed mental company to stay awake, so I started to recite the comedy routines of Dane Cook, Eddie Murphy, Brian Regan, Jerry Seinfeld and Jim Gaffigan. I knew every single track by heart, having listened to the same lineup through a 550-mile bike race in June, the Yukon River Quest in July and the Missouri River 340 paddling race in August, but for some reason knowing every line makes it even funnier.

Dawn broke clear and cold. An icy, biting wind caused my fingers to freeze in position around my paddle grips, and I shivered for hours, but I didn't stop. What good would that do, anyway? Then I'd still be cold and not break the record. At about 2:00 p.m., the clouds began to gather, and within the hour it was a full-blown epic storm. The headwinds and waves were so bad that Carter and I were reduced from averaging five or six miles per hour to averaging two. It was a battle of wills. At times I was paddling with everything I had and going backward. It wasn't any better on the downwind run. Whitecaps thrashed around us and threatened to tip us at any moment, and our boats were inexorably turned perpendicular to the wind. By 4:00 p.m., Carter knew that he would not break his existing record, so he called it a day, wisely choosing to save himself for a race the following weekend. I kept paddling because I knew I could break the women's record. I was nearly there already. I just had to keep my head in the game and my paddle in the water.

By 6:00 p.m., I could barely move my arms and was desperate to stay awake, so my friend Addie jumped into a kayak and came out to document my final hour on video. He's from Australia and quite a character, and he kept me engaged with silly interview questions and awake all the way through to exactly 7:30 p.m. Jeff sounded the air horn from the shore to indicate the official end of the record attempt. I laid my paddle across my lap, hung my head and just sat out there in the middle of the lake in the dark. Silent, grateful, happy, exhausted, alive, wrecked. I was done in every sense of the word. Addie attached a towline to the front of my boat and dragged me to shore. The GPS and Jeff's spreadsheet indicated that I had paddled exactly 121.37 miles, a new women's world record.

I lay on the floor of the shower that night with all of my gear on for the longest time, basking in the warmth of the beating water and dreaming. I couldn't shampoo my hair because I couldn't bring my arms up high enough or my head down low enough to make it work, but I didn't care.

Three weeks later I had a third brand-new metal hip and the joy of discovering a brand-new sport from the ashes of my old sawed-off and drilled-out bones. And life was good.

NEVER LET THE PURSUIT OF PERFECTION HINDER PROGRESS

As we've seen so far in this chapter, the most productive ways to deal with adversity are through out-of-the-box thinking, being courageous, becoming a visionary leader or shattering a norm. But sometimes the you-know-what hits the fan and the fan's on high speed, and all you can do is try to make the best art you can with the resulting splatter. Quite often the best way to get through is to laugh your way to the finish line. That's exactly what two teams did during the Eco-Challenge in Borneo.

Both teams, one from the United States and the other from the United Kingdom, started out with four people, but they each had two team members drop out along the way. The remaining four racers didn't want to quit the race after training so hard, spending so much money and traveling all the way to Borneo, so they asked event organizer Mark Burnett if they could form a new temporary team of four so they could continue the expedition. Burnett was vastly amused by these guys, so he gave them his blessing, and they were on their way as a new team of four.

After a few hours together, the team was interviewed on camera as they left for a long paddle. The captain of the new team announced, "We've now got a team of half US and half UK. We're the only team in the race now with mixed nationalities, so US and UK is U-SUK! And we suck!"

And off they went, laughing, bonded by adversity and poking fun at themselves for the next four days.

"The race is 320 miles long, and you can't change that," one of the American teammates said at the finish, "but to have good people around you and to have fun ... that's what it's all about. Doing it and laughing and getting through it."

Another teammate wisely declared, "Pain is mandatory, and suffering is optional." While many other teams fell by the wayside, Team U-SUK decided not to suffer and instead laughed all the way to the end, once again proving that crossing the finish line in any difficult endeavor is much more about who you are than what you know.

Yes, sometimes your day, week, year inevitably turns out to be a lot different than you had planned, but do you let that stop you? Your goal may be out of reach due to circumstances beyond your control, but that doesn't mean there isn't a finish line still out there for you. Oftentimes, the revised finish line ends up being just as meaningful as the original. The art of the leader who never lets the pursuit of perfection hinder progress is to find that new finish line, that new challenge to strive for, and to help the team see that light and reach for that star. World-class adversity managers know how to create a new win out of an old lose. They rewrite the rules for what it means to win, and mobilize their team toward that vision.

When it comes to leading through adversity, no team could match the brainstorming, uplifting, inspiring and visionary teammates I had in the 2000 Raid Gauloises. It was the sixth nonstop day of racing in the Himalayan peaks of Tibet and high deserts of Nepal, and the French were close on our heels. They were about two hours behind us when we came into a transition area where we were supposed to switch from hiking to mountain biking. All we had to do from there was pedal seventy miles through Nepal to the finish line, and we would win the Raid Gauloises, one of the world's most prestigious races, for the second year in a row. We were on a high as we approached the transition area after two long days on foot, as we expected to be received by our crew with cheers, hugs, warm food and ready gear for our triumphant ride to the finish. But our high ended quite abruptly when we discovered that our crew wasn't there. Neither were our bikes. The only people in the transition area were the French race organizers. We were shocked and in disbelief. That kind of thing had never happened to us before.

> **"WORLD-CLASS ADVERSITY MANAGERS REWRITE THE RULES FOR WHAT IT MEANS TO WIN."**

After scanning every corner of the transition area and hoping against hope that our crew was nestled snuggly in a tent sleeping, we finally had to admit that our worst nightmare had happened: no crew, no bikes, no way to win this race that we had battled for with our blood, tears and every ounce of our beings for the past six days. The French race organizer approached us and was, well . . . somewhat less than helpful, as he and his team of race organizers knew there was a French team about three hours behind us in second place. If you know anything about the French, they take it as a point of national pride to win.

"Where's our crew? What's going on?" we asked.

"This is not our problem. This is your problem," he replied. "They may be very far away, the crew. You are the only ones who have any problem. So, I don't know. Maybe you can sit and wait."

So we sat for about ten minutes, during which we all lamented our fate in staring silence, trying hard to grasp the enormity of it in our sleep-deprived brains. For six days we had been hopeful, then near the front of the pack, and then finally emerging as the team to beat, a team that was putting increasingly tiny bits of space between us and the teams behind with every step, every minute, every hour. Everything had been going perfectly, and we were being rewarded for our perseverance and synergy. But in the blink of an eye, all of that was over. We had gone from the heroic warriors of the sport to the team that was not only going to lose the race but was also now worried for the lives of the crew, one of whom was my fiancé, Jeff. I was walking around with my hands on my head muttering, "This is not happening, this is not happening," over and over.

Then something pretty miraculous happened in the face of this adversity. In the spirit of the great fire chief Alan Brunacini, who once said, "Change is the only thing that stays the same. It is our response to that change that dictates our success," three of my teammates, some of the most incredible leaders I have ever known, decided that the time for lamenting our losses was over and that as long as there was hope, we were still in the game. One of these leaders was Robert Nagle, a Harvard professor. Another was a doctor from New Zealand named Keith Murray. And then there was John Howard, a window washer from Christchurch, New Zealand. The best thing about John is that most of the time he looks like a bedouin wandering through the deserts and jungles of the world, wearing torn-up, fluorescent shorts from the '80s and refusing to put on a pair of socks. To complete the picture, he lives on top of a hill outside of Christchurch in a school bus. Yes, a real school bus. It's yellow. It says "SCHOOL BUS" on it. There is indeed a house-like structure on his property, but that's just where he keeps his race gear. I don't think John has ever taken a formal leadership course, yet he is one of the best natural leaders I have ever known.

"You know what? We're not going to just sit here and wait for the French to overtake us," John declared in his heavy Kiwi accent. "We've got to come up with a plan."

He started wandering around the outskirts of the transition area, motioning and pantomiming to the spectators who had gathered from the nearby village to watch a spectacle that they had never before seen and would never see again. It wasn't long before an idea hit him: we'd rent bikes from some of the locals! John began haggling with the spectators and came up with the five best bikes he could find. They were the crappiest bikes I'd ever seen—the spokes were sticking out, the seats were shredded with the stuffing coming out, the chains were rusted and the handlebars were upside down—but they rolled forward, so we didn't care how they looked. When John came back to the tent to tell us that he had a plan to get us to the finish line and asked us if we wanted to take a look, we seized that ray of hope and scrambled over to check out what the race gods had brought us. It wasn't pretty, but we had no other choice. At least we would be moving closer to our goal instead of giving the French team the thrill of coming into the transition and finding us there, in tears and devastated. We might go down, but at least we would go down swinging.

But the organizers weren't going to let us off the hook that easily. They told us that because the bikes didn't meet mandatory race specifications, like front shocks and mounted lights, we would be assessed a time penalty if we used them, to the tune of *three hours per bike!* We were stunned. They were not inspired by our "never say die" spirit. It was clear that they were not going to let us win and, worse, that they would even go so far as to continue to pile on ludicrous penalties to prevent it.

That's when Robert did something quite brave. In the television coverage, just as the race director was explaining to him that we would be penalized fifteen hours for our creative plan, Robert began giggling and then laughing hysterically, to the point where he fell on the ground and his legs flew up in the air. It was his way of telling the race director and all of the assembled media that the jig was up. This was the most ridiculous, laughable thing he had ever heard in his professional career, and now it was time to ignore this corrupt race and make our own way to the finish line.

Exhausted from the effort and shaking his head over the sheer disaster that this race had become, Robert made his way back to the rest of our team, still warily eyeing our new equipment. He told us what had happened and explained that the race director wasn't going to let us win, regardless of our heroic efforts. And then, just when we thought the hole of despair we found ourselves in couldn't get any deeper, he said something I will never forget. He told us, "Guys, we are the world champions. This isn't about the race anymore. This is about showing the sport and the world who *we* are as a team." Then he turned to the television cameras as he quickly gathered his gear and, with gravity behind every word and the light of a renewed mission sparkling in his eyes, he said, "Nothing will stop us."

In that moment we all embraced a new sense of purpose that transcended the race and the race director, who wasn't going to allow us to win his race for the second year in a row. It became our moment to show the world how true champions respond to adversity, and it caused us to rally and get our heads and hearts back into the game.

So we put on the only gear we had, which was whitewater rafting helmets and hiking shoes, and we got on those crappy bikes and rode out of that transition area with our heads held high. It wasn't pretty to watch, but we were back on the move, and that in itself felt great. I believe that despair and depression are often symptoms of a lack of action or an inability to make a decision. Once we had decided on a mission and were back on the move, our spirits were lifted.

"'IT'S IMPOSSIBLE,' SAID PRIDE. 'IT'S RISKY,' SAID EXPERIENCE. 'IT'S POINTLESS,' SAID REASON. 'GIVE IT A TRY,' WHISPERED THE HEART."
—unknown

I wish I could report that we had smooth sailing for those seventy miles of rough and sandy riding through Nepal, but I can't. The bikes had pretty much disintegrated by the time we got fifteen miles out of the transition area, and we had to resort to pushing them. We were trying to decide whether we wanted to push them the rest of the fifty miles to the finish line or just store them and walk, when suddenly, like an oasis on the desert, we saw our crew vehicle coming toward us with our super-sweet mountain bikes. We got on the radio and told the race director that our bikes had arrived; we were going to switch them out and have the old ones returned to the transition area.

"Oh no, that is not possible," he said. "You are not in an official transition area. You will be disqualified if you change the bikes on the course."

We stared at the radio, but not in disbelief anymore because we were all numb to the point where nothing could surprise or shock us now. It was simply the hundred-yard stare of mental, physical and spiritual exhaustion. So we had another tough decision to make: either push the bikes back fifteen miles or forward fifty. Once again our spirits were crushed. The high of riding rented bikes to the finish line was gone. At this point we all just wanted to disappear or shake ourselves awake from this nightmare. How many tough blows can a team take and still get up?

My favorite Japanese proverb is "fall down seven times, stand up eight." For each challenge we encounter in life, we must consciously choose to stand up or sit down. It's easy to tell yourself that something is too hard and give yourself an out or an excuse to sit down. But is it really too hard? In the arena of sports physiology, endurance athletes are told that our bodies are capable of twenty times more distance and effort than we believe they are. I wonder if the same isn't true of the mind and the spirit. It's only in the toughest of times that we find out what we're truly capable of. And in that way, these trials (mostly in retrospect, granted) are among the most valuable life lessons and character builders imaginable. I know that we discovered a lot about our teammates and ourselves somewhere between nothing and nowhere along the India–Nepal border that day.

Fall down seven times, stand up eight. So we stood up again. And turned around. And started pushing our bikes through the sand, back to the transition area that we had so triumphantly left several hours before. It was in that moment that Keith Murray, the doctor from New Zealand and one of the most winning racers in the history of the sport, stepped up to lead. He is a quiet man by nature, but he sensed the void of hope among his teammates and decided to try to rally us one more time. In the barren desert, through the deafening silence of our plodding footsteps in the deep sand, a singular and booming voice pierced the life-sucking 115-degree heat: "You know, people judge you in your life not by what you achieve, but what your attitude is for things." I still think of those words every single day. And I still can't believe that in our darkest time as a team, Keith was able to draw forth his highest thinking, most enlightened self. But that's what great leaders do.

Now, for entertainment value, I'll fill you in on the rest of the story. We didn't win that race. That would be too much of a fairy-tale ending, wouldn't it? But in true Hollywood-movie fashion, some form of justice prevailed in the end. Remember how I told you that there was a French team in second place? Well, as we were pushing our mountain bikes back to the transition area, to add insult to injury the French team that had been hours behind us was riding toward us at top speed on their high-tech mountain bikes toward the finish line. They passed us with a victorious flourish, cheering and high-fiving the cameramen and media as the pass of the American/Kiwi team was recorded for posterity on film. This was going to be incredible footage for the daily news in France. The French were on their way to winning the Raid Gauloises again, with the Americans and Kiwis in tears and ruin! *C'est du sport!* Then something amazingly karmic happened.

About five miles after the French team passed us, they were arrested and detained by the Nepalese police. I swear. You can't make this stuff up! To this day, we still don't know why. Wearing spandex in public, perhaps? Actually, it probably had more to do with Maoist terrorists and the detention of anyone who seemed out of place—and boy, were we adventure racers ever out of place. Needless to say, it was a complete train wreck at the end of that race, and a Finnish team that had been running six hours behind us at that last transition ended up tiptoeing through the mayhem and winning.

Here's the only saving grace for our team: at the awards ceremony when we were announced as the fourth-place finishers, we got a standing ovation, whereas the winners only got polite golf clapping. Keith was right. Above all else, people really do judge you by your attitude. It didn't make things all better, but to know that our colleagues knew what we had endured and that they acknowledged us as champions regardless of who crossed the line first was definitely consolation. Plus, that experience got us fired up for the next race, the Borneo Eco-Challenge, where "nothing would stop us," just as Robert had predicted.

ADVERSITY MANAGEMENT: A BUSINESS CASE STUDY

In the 1980s, Johnson & Johnson suffered a major blow when seven people died after ingesting Tylenol tablets that had been laced with cyanide. The tragedy was the result of criminal tampering that occurred in stores, outside of J&J's manufacturing facilities. But the company still accepted full responsibility for its product, issuing a nationwide recall of merchandise worth over $100 million. Instead of trying to cover up the problem and protect its reputation, J&J worked closely with the media, law enforcement, the medical community and the FDA to investigate the crime, keep consumers informed and develop new antitampering safeguards that would make Tylenol—and its competitors' products—safer. Although

Tylenol's market share plummeted initially, it wasn't long before it was once again the bestselling pain reliever in America.

Decades later, the J&J team's swift, candid, consumer-focused response to the Tylenol incident is still cited as a model for how companies ought to manage a crisis. Remember that the next time adversity crosses your team's path.

SYNERGY STARTERS: ADVERSITY MANAGEMENT

To inspire teamwork (and even better outcomes) when dealing with tough times and challenging issues:

Assemble a team of employees of similar rank (this can also be done via shared file system or intranet) or job description for a "Team Brainstorming Session." Ask each member of the team to take a piece of paper and at the top of the page write down a description of a "challenge" or tough issue he or she is experiencing at work. Then each team member passes the paper to the right and each member of the brainstorming team gets two minutes to read the issue and offer advice on ways to resolve it. People who are removed from the problem can often come up with ideas that we never considered, and it's also a great way to break down barriers and realize that we are not alone in our struggles and frustrations.

To remind your team of how they have dealt with and overcome adversity in the past and will prevail again:

Have each team member write down a "timeline" of their lives in years, with hash marks that denote times of major change or adversity (this doesn't have to be too personal and/or doesn't necessarily need to be shared with the team (for example, "team didn't win the contract," "discovered I had an illness" or "merger with..."). Then underneath that timeline, have them write how they managed that change, what they learned, how it made them stronger (or not) and what the eventual (hopefully positive) outcome was. Ask volunteers in the group to share a few of their stories of overcoming their obstacles or have small teams of two interview each other and then report the highlights of their partner's list to the larger group (so people won't feel shy about telling the team what a warrior they are!). This serves to remind people how resilient and resourceful they are in overcoming adversity and how sometimes a setback becomes the best thing that ever happened to them. They will walk away feeling a little more confident about the future and their ability to succeed against all odds.

To help your team focus on what it takes to "win" versus simply "not lose":

Have each person in the group write down what they perceive as two key factors to the short term success of your company (for example, "the successful launch of our new product" or "gaining 5% market share on the competition before the end of the 4th quarter.") Then, by vote, generate a consensus among the team about what they think the Top Three Key Success Factors are. Take each Key Success Factor and write it at the top of a single page on a flip chart. Then have two columns underneath that indicating "Win" and "Not Lose." Ask the team what "not losing" or holding ground looks like. Then brainstorm what it will take to truly win—no-holds-barred, out-of-the-box thinking without debate about whether it's possible. Finally, gain consensus on the top three ideas from the brainstorming session, research the possibility of executing the plan and meet again to discuss how to make it happen!

ELEMENT 4:

MUTUAL RESPECT

"Loyalty means not that I agree with everything you say, or that I believe you are always right. Loyalty means that I share a common ideal with you and, regardless of minor differences, we strive for it, shoulder to shoulder, confident in one another's good faith, trust, constancy and affection."

—**Dr. Karl Menninger**

I love Karl Menninger's quote because it reminds me of something so very important in life. We all talk about loyalty and trust, and how essential they are to a great team, but we often forget that loyalty and trust, like any aspects of an enduring relationship, need to be built and updated and cared for and maintained. Loyalty and trust are the platform on which everything else in the relationship will stand. Without that solid platform, built by day-to-day actions and not just feelings, your team will almost always deteriorate into individuals who just so happen to be walking in the same direction toward a common goal, and nothing more. Great team builders are those who are continually aware of both sides of this equation of mutual respect; that is, they are constantly proving through their actions that they've got your back, and they always believe (until proven otherwise) that you've got theirs. The best teams do everything in their power to take care of the most precious commodity a high performance team has: a one hundred percent solid bedrock of trust, loyalty and respect for and from their team members. How can we inspire that mutual respect every day?

REMEMBER THE ALUMINUM CAN THEORY

Alan Brunacini, the long-time chief of the Phoenix Fire Department, wrote something in an article that really stuck with me: "Anything you say in the heat of battle, when you're just looking to crush someone and go in for the kill, is like an aluminum can . . . it will stay in the environment forever." That is so true. All of us can remember something that someone once said to us during an argument or confrontation that caused such a deep wound that we will never forget it. Once those hurtful words are out floating around with the flotsam of the universe, they can never be taken back, and they will always remain. Sometimes it's just a chip off the bedrock of trust that you had, and sometimes it's a huge boulder. But in every case, your loyalty and trust are undermined.

Why do we let those aluminum cans come out of our mouths? To win. For our ego. To feel better in the moment because we have crushed the soul of someone and won the fight. A fantastic victory, right? Nope, never. That person will never feel the same way about you again. Your voice, saying those words, is playing on a rolling tape in their psyche forever. We all get frustrated, and we all want to scream or strangle somebody every now and then. But a great team builder will never let those aluminum cans out of his or her mouth. It's never worth it. Be the bigger person, be the graceful person, and the people around you will respect you even more.

Now, conversely, there are also positive aluminum cans, and those should be flying out of our mouths all the time. But strangely, as adults we're shy about doing that. Why is that? Why not tell a colleague how amazing she is or what a terrific job he did or how you really admire this or that about her? We're great when it comes to telling our kids these things, but hey, we adults are kids who just happened to get taller, grow more skin and put some life experience under our belts. We all love to hear why we're special or what other people think we're great at or how we've changed someone's life. Yet we so rarely hear it from anyone.

As a team builder, make it your mission to throw out at least one positive aluminum can every day to your teammates, and watch the bedrock of loyalty and trust strengthen and deepen. Throw one to your wife or husband, kids, colleagues, coaches, friends—all of them. If you are the light for people, a place where they feel good about themselves, you'll be amazed at the enduring bridges you'll be able to build.

MENTOR UNSELFISHLY

Another way to build trust and loyalty with teammates is to take them under your wing and show them the way to be better at the things you're good at. But in business, the barriers to this are often the compensation structure, in which individuals who do the same job function are ranked against one another or the desire to maintain the power that comes with knowing things that others don't.

So, let's take a look at both. On the surface, asking people to operate as a team or to share best practices when they are ranked against one another, which often happened when I was selling for a major pharmaceutical company, appears to fly in the face of logic, right? Yes and no. I encourage the business leaders with whom I've consulted to make the rewards system, or at least a component of it, match what people are asked to do. For example, if you want people to operate as a team, tie at least one component of their compensation or bonus plan to crossing a finish line together. That ought to encourage greater teamwork.

> **"SHARE YOUR RESOURCES AND MENTOR UNSELFISHLY. BE WARY OF PEOPLE WHO ATTACH STATUS TO KNOWING THINGS YOU DON'T."**
> —Chief Alan Brunacini, Phoenix Fire Department

I also have a different perspective on mentorship and how it can be an asset to any team, even if employees are ranked as individuals. I discovered this little nugget of wisdom from Steve, a colleague in pharmaceutical sales. Steve was ranked as our number one sales rep year in and year out. That boggled my mind because at the end of every week, he would send the other two hundred of us a little update, in which he would tell us about what worked well for him that week, how he overcame an objection or to give us the scoop about a recent study that shed some new light on why our product was superior to our competitors'. I incorporated some of Steve's ideas and just moved on with my life, thinking, *Wow, I'm grateful for the heads-up each week, but how is Steve going to maintain his number one spot if he keeps sharing all of his best stuff?*

I was so curious about it that I set out to get an answer at our next national meeting. When I saw Steve at dinner, I sidled up to him and after a few minutes of the standard "connecting to the person before the point," I started digging for answers to the conundrum.

"Hey, how is it that every week you tell us all your best tips and tricks, yet you're still able to stay a mile ahead of us at the end of the year?"

"Well, I do like to help people," Steve replied, "but the truth is that it helps my numbers, too."

I responded with the Scooby Doo sound that allowed a baffled dog to ask questions: "Hrrrrrrumphhhhh?"

Steve laughed and said, "What do you think happens every week when I send out those tips? I get a dozen or so tips back from other people from all around the country, and then I incorporate their ideas into my sales calls and meetings. And together, this little circle of twenty or thirty regulars who give and take information from one another have just spiraled up the rankings together. Haven't you ever noticed that the same twenty or so people are always at the top of the list? That's them."

My brain hurt, as did my little competitive soul. All of these people got better by sharing, by mentoring one another? I had spent my whole life as a student covering up my answers with my arm (and in some cases, the rest of my body) so nobody else could see them. This was madness! But over time it made a lot more sense. By growing this brotherhood and sisterhood of people who unselfishly mentored one another, they all got better and generated a huge lead over the rest of the competition. Steve showed them respect by sharing the keys to his success, and they, in receiving his gift, gave it back in spades.

A rising tide lifts all boats.

ACTING LIKE A TEAM IS MORE IMPORTANT THAN FEELING LIKE A TEAM

Ok, let's tell the truth. This team building stuff is awesome, and it's a lofty goal. It springs from accessing our most divine and enlightened selves, but sometimes we frankly just want to trip each other in the hallway. Don't worry! It's totally normal to think that way. What isn't normal is thinking that we're always going to feel all fluffy and bunnies and rainbows and flowers and big purple dinosaurs when we're around one another.

The best team builders understand that regardless of what we feel in the moment, it's much more important to act like the teammate or leader we aspire to be. I can't tell you how many times each day I ask myself, *How would Lance Armstrong lead his team through this?* or *How would my dad* (the smartest man on Earth. For real. Just ask him. Ha!) *handle this?* and then act accordingly. If you act the part of a great teammate or a great leader for long enough—in other words, fake it 'til you make it—the good feelings between you and your teammates will come back. Trust me, it never fails.

Before we started the 1998 Raid Gauloises in Ecuador, my teammates and I agreed that if we were ever struggling or having issues with one another during the race, we would never let anyone outside our circle know it. Whatever happened would stay within our team. It was a good thing we made that pact before leaving the starting blocks because we had an ugly situation develop at one point.

Ian and John, our two navigators, began arguing with each other about the right way to go around one particular mountain. They finally came to an impasse in their ultra-polite haggling about the route, and John, being the more stubborn of the two, said, "Well all right then, I'm going to go this way," and he took off in that direction.

Then Ian said, "Well, all right then, I'm going to go *that* way," and he took off and started walking in the other direction. My remaining teammates and I ran back and forth between Ian and John, wondering which one we ought to follow. Eventually we all split up, which is really bad juju in adventure racing because you have no idea where you're all going to end up. But the funny part of the story is that each group went its own way around the mountain, certain in the conviction that theirs was the only right way to go, and we all met back up on the other side!

Then we were all pissed off at one another. But because we had made that pact of never letting anyone outside our circle know that we were struggling, when we got to the next transition area, Robert Nagle said, "Remember, we are the world champions. Act like it." And we all immediately switched into "I love you; you're my greatest teammate" mode:

"Hey, can I help you out, mate?"

"Aw, yeah! I'd appreciate that!"

"Here, let me help you get your shoes on."

"Can I get you some food, mate?"

"You were so strong in that last leg!"

"You look great!"

"You're the man!"

"No, *you're* the man!"

We acted as though we were all best friends having the most excellent race of our lives. We acted as if nothing was going to stop us. And then something happened. As soon as we started treating one another like teammates again, we actually started to feel like teammates again. Then we were right back in the flow. We left the transition area with all the other teams' ground crews believing that we were unstoppable, a tight, cohesive, happy unit on a mission to win. That's exactly what we wanted them all to report to their teams as they entered the transition area. We were back on track as a team for the rest of the race, which we won—in part because we knew the importance of acting like great teammates even when we didn't feel like it.

> **"I ALWAYS PREFER TO BELIEVE THE BEST IN EVERYBODY; IT SAVES SO MUCH TROUBLE."**
> —Rudyard Kipling

BELIEVE BEYOND REASON

Part of the art of mutual respect is the power we give to our teammates when we believe in them beyond reason. What happens to people when we believe in them? They will often rise to the occasion to prove us right. The opposite is true as well. If we treat people as though they are not worthy of our respect, they will often find a way to prove us right.

My teammates in Ecuador believed in me far beyond reason when it came time to climb that ice-covered, 19,700-foot Cotopaxi volcano (I lived at sea level and wasn't adjusted to altitude, not to mention my being the newest and most inexperienced person on the team), but that belief in me is what gave me the power, physically and mentally, to get to the top. With every step I thought, *I can't let them down,* and pictured Robert's hopeful face looking down into mine, trying to give me the confidence I needed to stop crying, stand up and get to the top of the mountain.

Give it a try with the teammates in your life: your friends, employees, colleagues and family. Show them that you believe in them and that you trust them, and watch them do everything in their power to not let you down.

GIVE RESPECT AS A GIFT, NOT AS A GRADE

From the time we're little kids, we learn that the way we behave will either earn or diminish the respect that our family, teachers and friends give us. As adults we do the same thing: for the most part, we stand back and make other people earn our respect. But to become a world-class team, I urge you to grant respect to your teammates right off the bat. Don't make them prove themselves first. Give respect as a gift, not as a grade, because it really bonds your team when you do.

The power of receiving respect as a gift and not a grade hit home for me many years ago, right after I graduated from the San Diego Fire Department academy. In San Diego, new firefighters spend their first year out of the academy on probation, which means that the department can fire them at any moment. To ensure that everyone knows that you're a "probie," the department puts a bright orange shield on your helmet—a shield that might as well be a flashing neon sign that says, *"Moron . . . moron . . . moron"*—which makes it easy for every other firefighter to identify you from a distance so they can all watch you screw stuff up for their daily amusement.

For my first week out of the fire academy, I was assigned to work with a captain who was known far and wide as being a crusty guy. You know the type: an older, semi-caveman firefighter who doesn't really want women on the job. I was petrified. First thing that morning, he told our crew that we were going to have a drill on a piece of equipment called the gated Y. I was thrilled that we were going to focus on the Y because I knew exactly how that particular piece of equipment worked. The gated Y is a steel hose adapter shaped like a forked snake tongue, or the letter *Y*. You attach a large-diameter hose to the receiving end, and the gated Y adapter splits the water into two smaller outlets to which you can attach hose lines. There is a toggle switch on top of the Y between the two outlets so you can control which of the smaller outlets you'd like the water to flow to. We use this for structure fires when we may be fighting fire on two different sides of a building.

My job on the drill was simple: attach the hose lines to the Y and make sure that the toggle was pointing the right way to make the water come out of the right side of the Y, since we had attached a hose and nozzle only to that right-hand side. The left side of the Y was just left open with no hose attached. My partner for the day was in the ready position on the end of the hose line, nozzle in hand. I moved the toggle to the right on the Y and yelled back toward the fire engine, "Ready for water!" to which the engineer responded, "Water coming!"

When water shoots down one of those large-diameter hoses, it's scary. It's like those giant caterpillars in the movie *Dune* rolling along under the sand. It makes a lot of noise, and it's shooting right at you at top speed. As I watched the hose come to life, coursing with a great rush of pressurized water, I froze in a swirling panic of self-doubt: *Which way is the toggle supposed to go again? I have it switched to the right, but does that mean the water is going to go to the right, or am I cutting off the supply of water to the right...? Ugh!*

At the penultimate moment, as the powerful rush of water approached the gated Y, I changed my mind. I bent down and switched the toggle over to the left-hand side, which was the side with the open hole. You can see the resulting circus coming a mile away, right? The water shot out the left-hand side of the gated Y and hit me so hard on the side of my leg that it knocked me off my feet. Suddenly I'm rolling around on the ground getting pummeled by water, black-and-blue marks springing up all over my body, and I wasn't even smart enough to run away. My captain literally had to yell, "Run away! Run away!" *Hey, great idea!* I said to myself as I slowly made my way up onto my feet in eighty pounds of soaking wet fire gear and dragged my soggy butt to a dry corner of the drill ground, mortified. In the background, I heard the captain yelling to the engineer to shut down the pump.

When I finally had the courage to look up, everyone on the crew was standing there staring at me, this pathetic, soaking wet pro-bie doofus. As I slowly shuffled my way back to the captain, I distinctly remember holding my arms at my sides at attention, which is pretty funny in retrospect. I guess I just wanted to get fired at attention.

"Sir, can I please respectfully request that we do the drill again, sir?" I asked. "I'm pretty sure I've got it now."

"Nope," he said, shaking his head. "We're just going to shut down and go home." He turned on his heel and walked toward his seat on the engine.

I was dying inside. I really wanted that job. It was my dream to be a firefighter. I wanted another chance to prove to the captain that I could handle it. I ran after him, still at attention.

"Please sir, could you please stop, sir? I respectfully request that we do this drill again, sir."

As he turned to face me, I could see that he was fighting to hold back a grin while still clinching his ever-present toothpick between his teeth. "We don't need to do the drill again, Ben-a-casa."

On the verge of tears and with my voice cracking, I got up the nerve to ask, "Can I please ask why, sir? I really want this job."

He removed the toothpick and responded with something I'll never forget: "All right, Ben-a-casa, I'll tell ya why. Ya see, it was my goal when I woke up this morning that by the end of the day, a firefighter on my crew would know how that gated Y works better than anybody on the job. And I'm pretty sure that at this moment you know how that thing works better than anybody in the goddamned *world*." Then he stuck his little toothpick back in the corner of his mouth and strutted off, immensely pleased with himself.

At lunch I thanked him for the way he had handled my blunder during the drill.

"Look, I know you're not an idiot," he said, smiling as much as a tough guy was allowed. "Besides, that was just damn good entertainment for me and the boys. You can come to work for me anytime."

My captain gave me the gift of respect on my first day on the job, respect that I certainly hadn't earned. That was the kind of leader I wanted to work with. As soon as I got off probation, I requested to be assigned to his crew, much to the amazement of most of my colleagues, and I had the honor of working with him for the next seven years until he retired. Giving me respect as a gift and not a grade showed me who this great leader was at his core. I have spent the rest of my career trying to live up to his belief in me.

MUTUAL RESPECT:
A BUSINESS CASE STUDY

In 1962, the late Sam Walton founded his company, Walmart, around three core beliefs: excellence, customer service and respect for the individual. There is an entire page on Walmart's corporate website devoted to personal stories from company employees, known as associates, that illustrate the many ways that Walton showed his respect for his team members. Here's a story from an associate in Personnel named Lisa:

> *I had worked at Walmart for a year in 1990 when the Eagan, Minnesota Walmart was opening. I worked the overnight shift then and apparently it was customary for Mr. Sam to give a Texan Barbeque for the associates who helped open a new store.*
>
> *We all knew we would be fed, but to my surprise up rolled a limo with Sam and some board members*

> *with him along with the food that was promised.*
> *He and those with him served all of the over-*
> *night associates at 2 am [sic] in the morning.*[3]

Walton's respectful way of interacting with the people on his team was legendary. Indeed, it was one of the keys to his success. It helped him grow Walmart from one little discount store in Arkansas into a global retail giant staffed with thousands of loyal associates, and a 2010 revenue of over $400 billion. Who says nice guys have to finish last?

SYNERGY STARTERS: MUTUAL RESPECT

Whenever the warm feelings escape you or you need to respond to a challenge within your team, ask yourself this question: *What would I do right now if I were the person that my ___ believes I am?* Fill in the blank with someone who loves you unconditionally and always assumes the best about you. It could be your mom, dad, son, daughter, sister, brother, spiritual leader or dog. Let the answer to that question guide you toward being a world-class teammate. It works every time.

To breed mentorship among people with similar job descriptions and goals:

- Create a simple quarterly contest (for example, "Overcoming

---

3   Walmart, "When I Met Mr. Sam," http://walmartstores.com/AboutUs/332.aspx (accessed October 2, 2011).

Objections" or "Sales Success!" or "You're Not Gonna Believe This!" or whatever you'd like your staff to share information about), and create a shared intranet page where colleagues share a story about an objection they overcame or something creative they did to close a sale, etc. Award the top three stories each week with fun prizes and let everyone know that the most impactful stories and most prolific contributors will be recognized at your company's largest annual meeting.

To promote respect for one another's job duties and responsibilities by walking a mile in their shoes:

- Ask each team member to write a one-page "Week in the Life" that illustrates exactly what that person does in a given day/week and the outcomes for which they are responsible (this can also be done interview style with a partner if team members are in the same office). Also have them answer the following four questions at the end of their narrative:

  1. What is the biggest misconception about what I do?
  2. What do I wish more people understood about my job/responsibilities?
  3. What is the toughest thing about my job?
  4. What is the best part of my job?

There will be many surprises, as assumptions about one another and what we actually do all day are rarely accurate. Everyone will leave with a deeper appreciation for one another as well as a true appreciation for their own jobs.

To help employees understand and appreciate the uniqueness of everyone in the room and how they think/learn/adapt:

- Have everyone in the room grab an 8-½ x 11 piece of paper and tell them to close their eyes, hold the paper in front of their face and follow your instructions exactly. Then instruct them to "fold the paper in half," then "tear off the top right corner," then "fold the paper in half again," then "tear off the bottom left corner," then "fold the paper in half one more time" and finally "tear out the bottom middle section." After that, announce that when you count to three, everyone should open their eyes, unfold their "snowflake" and see if anyone else in the room has the same one. Trust me, in a room full of a couple thousand people, you won't find two that are the same. It's fun to watch people hold up their snowflakes and laugh at the fact that they're so different! This exercise makes two points: First, everyone processes things differently based on their background, education, experience and so on. Although as the leader you give the same exact instructions to everyone, the result is as varied as the people in the room. Are any of them wrong? Nope. This exercise reinforces the fact that just because someone doesn't do things the way you would doesn't make them wrong—it's just processed through a different and usually no less capable mind. Second, if you want something completed per your *exact* specifications, you need to be a lot clearer about the directions, specifications and expected outcomes. Quite often leaders get frustrated because they "told them exactly what to do" and the result is often pretty far off from your personal vision. As leaders you either need to be extremely clear and not expect people to read your mind, or you have to applaud your employees' individual snowflakes when they're presented to you.

ELEMENT 5:

WE THINKING

"It's amazing what can be accomplished when nobody cares who gets the credit."

— unknown

In the early days of adventure racing, most teams tried to recruit the best mountain biker, the best paddler, the best navigator and so on and then organize them into a team. More often than not, these teams of individual superstars wouldn't even see the halfway point of the race, much less the finish. Too many egos and too little sharing of strengths and weaknesses was most often the culprit. It wasn't until my group realized that being a true team builder was the most important skill to have in the long haul that we started to win races. I'm convinced that the same holds true for teammates throughout the rest of our lives.

In the real world, it's easy to be an island, to pay lip service to teamwork and to get to the finish line of a project alone if you need to. We mostly rely on our own talents, wits and skills because they have gotten us this far, haven't they? But to get to the next level, beyond what you can accomplish alone, you must be able to build and inspire a "We Thinking" team in which you share strengths and weaknesses, integrate various talents and skills, and see yourself as just one important piece of a high-performance puzzle.

STRIVE TO TAKE EVERYONE ACROSS THE FINISH LINE TOGETHER

When I made the switch from Ironman triathlons to adventure racing, it was quite a culture shock. In a triathlon, you're on an individual journey, and you go as fast as you can go, slow down when you need to and speed up if you're feeling good. It's the simple life, with only yourself to count on and only yourself to blame. But when I started adventure racing, the concept of winning as an individual became a thing of the past. I learned quickly that on the world's best teams, you don't covet and conserve your strength; you offer it to the team. Most important, when you aren't feeling great, you offer your weakness and suffering to the team as well. The idea of collective assets (strength, gear, food) versus mine and yours is a key tenet of We Thinking.

In our real lives and from a young age, we're wired to think of winning as being a mutually exclusive thing: if I am to win, everyone else must lose. But once we've decided who is on our team (is it just you against the world every day, or do you consider your family, your business unit, your clients or your entire company as part of your team? This is an important question, one that we have to think about and answer every single day), why can't we then strive to take all of our teammates onto the top of that podium with us? Does it somehow make us *less than* to have our teammates with us as we cross that finish line? I submit that as a leader and a team builder, it makes you *more than.* Isn't it more fun and memorable to have a Stanley Cup–style finish, with everyone pouring champagne on one another on stage, than to have an Olympic-style awards ceremony where you're standing on that podium alone?

ACCEPT RESPONSIBILITY FOR SUCCESS AND FAILURE AS A TEAM

Whenever we saw a team in which there was finger-pointing at one another, we knew that particular team was never going to make it to the finish line no matter how great the individual members were as athletes. Rumblings like, "I don't think Bob trained enough. He's been lying to us the whole time" or "Steve really blew the navigation in that section" give the signal that individuals will be thrown under the bus on this team, so it's every man or woman for his or herself. If this pointing out of individual weaknesses or mistakes continues, especially in public, you can wave goodbye to team unity and the desire to work *for* your teammates versus protecting yourself from them.

To that end, the best teams word everything as *we:* "We lost our way." "We struggled in that section." "We lost the account." The people who are responsible feel bad enough already. And more than likely, they know who they are. They will appreciate you having their back, and in the future, when the shoe is on the other foot, they will have yours. What happens on the team stays on the team. This grace and generosity of spirit is the glue that holds a team together over the long haul.

Besides, many team issues are due to a lack of synergy and not a particular individual's performance. For example, if an adventure racing team's navigation is wrong, it is not because a single navigator screwed up. There are three other people who are supposed to be helping that navigator along the way. His job is to communicate which landmarks you should all be looking for, and the rest of the team should be vigilantly backing him up: "Steve, I see that ridgeline you told us to look for, and I think I see that little meadow coming up, too." It's that constant communication that keeps people thinking as a team.

On high-performance teams, everyone accepts complete responsibility for the group's successes and failures. Allowing even one person to fail is a breakdown of the entire team because everyone should have been pitching in to help the one who was struggling. Conversely, if someone is having difficulty and keeps it to themselves, they're not a We Thinking person either.

> **"ON HIGH-PERFORMANCE TEAMS, EVERYONE ACCEPTS COMPLETE RESPONSIBILITY FOR THE GROUP'S SUCCESSES AND FAILURES."**

SUFFER EQUALLY

The best team builders are consistently thinking of ways to make the team as a whole move more quickly and efficiently, and for us that involves tinkering with our collective strengths and weaknesses until we're suffering equally. The first time I heard the term *suffer equally* was at the starting line of the Raid Gauloises in Ecuador, my first race with the best team in the world. Right before the start, our team captain, John Howard, told us to put all of our gear in the middle of our circle. Then, he carefully meted out who should take which pieces of gear based on the weight of that gear and each person's capabilities in the first seventy-five-mile run (at 14,000 feet, ugh). I watched in horror as John handed our strongest runners, Robert Nagle and Steve Gurney, almost all of my gear, leaving me with just a water bladder and some Cheetos in my pack. I was mortified. It was obvious that I was carrying much less gear than the other top women.

"Hey, I'm pretty embarrassed here," I said to John. "Can I get some of my gear back? The other women are carrying their own weight."

"Well, the other women aren't going to win this race, are they?" he replied. "Look, when we start running off this start line at 14,000 feet, your heart rate with all of your own gear is going to be 160 to 170. Robert's will be 120. Doesn't it make sense for both of you to move forward at about 140? We'll go a heck of a lot longer without anyone falling apart if we try to suffer equally."

He was absolutely right. As soon as that starting gun went off, Robert was running like the wind, even with the extra weight, and I was grateful to be able to keep up with the team for longer than I would have if I were carrying all my gear. He and I were truly suffering equally. Throughout that entire race, we tracked our effort levels on a number system every hour or so. I had never seen this done before. Someone would yell out, "Where are we on the 1-to-10 scale?" and everyone would throw out a number, with 10 being "I feel perfect!" and 1 being "Stick a fork in me." If we were all within that 5–8 range, we would keep moving with no changes. If someone dipped below 5, with anyone else on the team reporting 7 or over, we would quickly shuffle gear around or have the suffering person give up their pack completely. This was all done without ego or fear of repercussions. It simply meant moving forward on the course as a team as fast as we could.

A win lasts forever. Suffering is temporary and will most likely be forgotten if you make it onto the podium. In fact, most of my stronger teammates appreciate it when egos are left at the starting line and their help is accepted and appreciated. They want to suffer equally because that's the key to winning. The other important thing to remember is that in any long-term, worthwhile journey with a team, in business and in life, we will at some point be the strongest link and the weakest link. A We Thinking team accepts that and minimizes the impact of it for the greater good. There is a beautiful flow of giving and accepting on world-class teams, and it's an uplifting experience to be a part of it.

YOUR PROBLEMS = MY PROBLEMS

On a We Thinking team, all problems are *our* problems. All success is *our* success. All failure is *our* failure. Along those same lines, you will rarely hear, "That's not my job" or "That's not my problem" from the world's best. Although you may have had nothing to do with an issue that befalls a teammate, in adventure racing their problem is your problem because you can't progress to the finish line without them. In the real world, we can definitely move forward on our course without helping one another. But as solo players, we can't match the outcomes that a great team can accomplish together. A good deal of that success has to do with not only sharing strengths but also, and most important, sharing the good, the bad and the not so pretty circumstances that each individual is enduring.

This approach to teamwork acted in our favor time and time again. During one race, I lost a pedal off a mountain bike in the middle of nowhere. I wasn't able to screw it back in; the thing was completely stripped and just kept falling out. If I had been on almost any other team, my teammates would have been shaking their heads, saying, "Wow, too bad. It sucks to be you." But on this extreme team, everyone was off their bikes in a flash, helping me find a solution. We were in an open field looking around every nook and cranny for a stick that might work or a piece of rebar or something we could use to re-create a pedal. The lost pedal was our problem as a team. No one left me there to figure it out on my own while they sat down and had lunch or, worse yet, went on without me. No, the attitude was that it was our bike and therefore our problem.

Eventually we decided that we were wasting more time looking for a solution than just dealing with the situation, so for the last sixty miles of that segment, the three strongest guys took thirty-minute turns rotating onto that bike. It was the job of the other strong teammates to ride alongside the crippled bike and put two fingers on that rider's lower back to help push them up the hills because that person was working twice as hard as everyone else. It became my job to remind everybody to drink and to hand out energy bars to keep them fed because they were so focused on pushing and towing and riding on one leg that they were forgetting their upkeep.

That's the way a We Thinking team tackles a problem: they turn it into a team building challenge. And that's exactly what we did when a teammate lost his paddle during the rafting section of the Raid Gauloises in Argentina. We were two days into the race, paddling like crazy down a river on a big raft, when a teammate's paddle got hung up on a rock and was snatched out of his hands. There was no way to retrieve it because there's no going backward in whitewater.

My teammate didn't want to be up the proverbial creek without a paddle for the whitewater segment, so we decided to pull over and look for a paddle substitute, anything we could use to help propel the raft down the river. There wasn't much. The only piece of wood we could find was a sapling—a small tree, really—with a fanned-out section at the bottom that was sort of similar to a paddle. In addition to looking irretrievably stupid, it also weighed about fifteen pounds. Obviously our teammate couldn't use it for more than a few minutes at a time, so for the remaining hours of paddling, we passed around that sapling, which we called the Hammer of Thor. Each of us got the Hammer of Thor for about ten minutes until our arms exploded, and then we handed it off to the next guy. That way we shared the burden and were able to continue pursuing our common goal.

> **"THROUGHOUT OUR BEST, MOST MEMORABLE RACES, SHARING WAS TAKEN TO THE EXTREME."**

Throughout our best, most memorable races, sharing was taken to the extreme. We knew it was a good race when, as we unpacked all of our disgusting, wet, muddy, smelly gear, there would be a constant parade back and forth between our hotel rooms to deliver one another's gear back to the rightful owner. Throughout a successful race effort, instead of stopping to put gear back into our own packs after we used it, we were always putting our gear or food into someone else's pack, which was much more easily accessible while we were running. So by the end of the race, we would have little of our own gear in our packs and random bits of everyone else's. It didn't matter whose it was at the time because it was all ours. In fact, we discovered that we could move a lot faster if our food and gear were strategically located in a teammate's pack, which we could access without stopping or contorting ourselves. Tricks of the trade. To this day, I have a lot of little pieces of gear in my garage with all of my teammates' initials, things I found after the fact and was instructed to not bother returning. Each is a fond memory of a race well run. I know my teammates have plenty of my stuff in their garages, too.

DON'T COMPARE, COMPETE OR CRITICIZE

We Thinkers cut out the gossip, the negativity and the backstabbing on their team. This starts with you, and trust me, your team will follow. Consciously catch yourself if you are comparing, competing with or criticizing your teammates. Nothing ruins the spirit of a team faster.

Instead of being a C3 teammate—that is, one who compares, competes and criticizes—I urge you to try to be an A3 teammate: a person who accepts, acknowledges and appreciates the positive things about his or her teammates. This attitude will get you a heck of a lot closer to the finish line and help you move through those checkpoints a whole lot faster, too. Remember that we work for people, not for companies. Everyone will work much harder for an A3 teammate or leader than a C3 one.

One of the most counterproductive C3 team disasters I've ever seen came during the 2002 Eco-Challenge in Fiji, when one particular leader fostered eating up his team from the inside out because he tolerated and personally engaged in comparing, competing and criticizing to feed his own ego. It was bad. These guys had an all-you-can-eat buffet on each other by the time their race was over—and their race was over in about thirty-six hours because they completely self-destructed.

> **"AN A3 TEAMMATE:
> A PERSON WHO ACCEPTS,
> ACKNOWLEDGES AND
> APPRECIATES THE
> POSITIVE THINGS ABOUT
> HIS OR HER TEAMMATES."**

The leader was an army Ranger whom his female teammate called Ranger Boy, and the rest of the team was made up mostly of elite Special Forces types, including a navy SEAL. Ironically, the team was racing on behalf of a charity. They were racing together for a higher purpose, yet they treated one another like enemies. Historically, military teams do not do well in adventure racing because the top-down leadership style isn't what is called for when there's no real battle plan to execute. In adventure racing, the plans change minute to minute, and no one person can be an expert. You've got to accept that you personally won't have the answers to handle everything, but instead trust that you have a team that can handle just about anything. But Ranger Boy was the anti–We Thinker. He was one of those people who must have total control of his team at all times, who must take full credit and be the smartest guy in the room. For his own ego's sake, he had to be the hero who was going to get everybody to the finish line. He took a potential We Thinking team and destroyed it with C3 Thinking.

The team's extremely short race began when they started to gang up on their lone female member, whom I'll call Debi. One racer even said that he believed Debi had lied about her fitness level. Another blamed her because they had to move slower than he liked. But when Debi asked her teammates to take some of her gear to make the strength-to-weight ratio more even and allow her to move faster, which is what all We Thinking teams do at the beginning of a race, Ranger Boy took bits and pieces from her pack, threw them to one of the other strong racers and said with a smirk, "Here, take this, it don't weigh nothin.'" Instead of extending a hand to their teammate, they decided to criticize Debi for asking for help. Her spirit was crushed.

One teammate down, two left to destroy. The team had barely gotten through that when one of its rookie members, whom I'll call Mark, became obsessed with proving to Ranger Boy how strong he was. Mark rushed ahead of his teammates even though they warned him that he would soon burn out if he kept going full throttle. Instead of climbing a waterfall or ridge via the easiest route alongside his teammates, Mark would specifically choose the hardest possible route so everyone would have to stop and look at him. Mark was essentially yelling, "Notice me! Notice me!" and his team captain was essentially saying, "Not in a million years, buddy." Each time Mark tried to impress his leader, Ranger Boy took it as a personal affront and concluded that Mark was only trying to outdo him. As a result, Ranger Boy decided to crush Mark.

"I told (Mark) . . . I haven't made it difficult for you yet," Ranger Boy said, with television cameras rolling. "If you really want to push and make this race hard, I can make you physically push yourself to drop."

Wait, what? Aren't these guys supposed to be on the same team?

As a result of Ranger Boy's lack of empathy and understanding of his role as a leader and Mark's desperate desire to be recognized, Mark ended up completely frying himself and became the team's weakest link. He had a total physical meltdown—and all of this happened in the first thirty-six hours of the race.

A We Thinking captain could have solved Debi's and Mark's problems in 0.2 seconds flat, but instead Ranger Boy made the division deeper by fanning the criticism. He forgot to leave his ego at the starting line. He wouldn't allow anyone on the team but himself to be strong. Instead of threatening to push his teammate until he dropped, a We Thinking captain would have said, "Mark, you're such an incredible athlete, and you're so strong. Why don't you take Debi's pack, and we'll all go together? And look at how amazing you are, Debi. Now you're keeping up!" He could have chosen to treat Mark's desire for recognition and Debi's willingness to ask for help as benefits, but instead he chose to treat them as personal affronts to his undisputed title as the strongest and most omnipotent person on the team.

As shocking as this was to watch on television, and as much as everyone giggles at the prospect of someone so shortsighted and egotistical, you would be surprised at the number of people who come up to me after I've shown a clip of this team during my presentation and tell me that they're pretty sure they work with Ranger Boy or, worse, that they see a little too much Ranger Boy in themselves. We all want to be recognized as the strong one, the smart one, the powerful one—it's human nature. Ranger Boy's team was giving all of that to him, but he didn't see it. In this case, nobody was disputing his leadership, his strength or his experience. They just wanted his acknowledgment that they were strong and capable and smart, too.

Why is that so hard for people to do? Why wouldn't this leader give his teammates what they needed? For starters, he had a lack of confidence in his leadership role. Second, he had a lack of understanding of who his team was. In this case, his only teammate was himself. In his narrow view, everyone walking beside him was his competitor, even though keeping them together and motivated was the only way to achieve his goal of crossing the finish line. And third, he had a disregard for We Thinking. He allowed and instigated comparing, competing and criticizing among his teammates instead of shutting it down. It never crossed his mind to put Mark's strength together with Debi's need and allow them to suffer equally for the good of the team. What a shame. He completely missed an opportunity to lead in a way that would have elevated everyone.

SEEK SYNERGY EVERYWHERE

Creating synergy isn't always about victoriously propelling a team to the finish line. Believe it or not, synergy can also be the key to *individual* victory when the situation calls for it. Creating short-term team synergy to vault oneself into the lead has been standard practice in sports for years, but it is a rare thing indeed to find people in the business world using this strategy. In general, in our day-to-day business lives, we're concerned with our own goals, getting the credit we deserve, how much we impress the people around (and especially above) us on the food chain. I get it. It's all based on the ways in which we're rewarded, and it makes sense for people to modify their behavior to get that promotion pellet or pat on the back. But even within those parameters of individual effort and reward, We Thinking should not be overlooked as a strategy. For example, in both adventure racing and bike racing, we often bond together and share information and resources with our biggest competitors for our personal gain. Seems counterintuitive, you say? Let me explain.

In the first several days of a six-to-ten-day adventure race, a lot of the game involves going as far as you can on the course during the day because it's exponentially more difficult and laborious to tackle complex navigation and terrain at night. If you can get a jump on the bulk of the field in the early going and force the majority of the field behind you to do the tough parts at night, the gap between the front teams and the rest of the race gets wider and wider, and therefore your competitors become fewer and fewer. So in an effort to "make the break" on the rest of the field and limit the number of potential contenders as you get closer to the finish line, the most experienced racers have learned that cooperation with the other top teams is critical. The power struggle begins right off the starting line, with the fastest teams trying to shed the long line of competitors who are simply following in their wake and not using any energy to make the navigational decisions. By twenty-four hours in, there are usually only five to seven teams left in the front pack, either real contenders or those that are completely strung out and hanging on by a thread. That's when the real race begins.

At this point, something surprising often happens. Generally, at a crucial navigational point where there is great potential for error or where a group effort will behoove everyone, the true contenders for the win (we know who we are!) will often silently declare a truce and form an alliance to work together. We will share maps, figure out the bits of tough navigation together, draft one another on the bikes or boats, share food; in essence, we create a little cluster of potential winners who use one another to create an even bigger gap on the rest of the field. This small group of teams, usually two or three, will work together like a pod of whales gathering krill until that gap between us and the chase pack is too great to be bridged. Minute by minute, we use our collective talents and strengths to close the door on the chasers. This can last anywhere from one to three days. Once we are assured that the winning team will definitely be one of us in the lead pack, the energy switches. Slowly but perceptibly, it's "game on" again as the finish line comes within range. The last twenty-four hours or so is a gruesome battle for the win against other teams we respect and honor, but who are going to have to settle for second place! Ha!

> "IN HELPING OTHERS, WE SHALL HELP OURSELVES, FOR WHATEVER GOOD WE GIVE OUT COMPLETES THE CIRCLE AND COMES BACK TO US."
> —Flora Edwards

The We Thinking fun doesn't have to stop for a solo event either. In 2006, after twelve years away from the sport of triathlon, I decided to try another Ironman just for fun. The Ironman is a multisport endurance race consisting of a 2.4-mile swim, 112-mile bike ride and a 26.2-mile marathon run. I had completed seven of them in the early 1990s (wow, I'm old!) and thought it would be a fun way to train for my next adventure race.

But somewhere in the middle of the bike ride, I realized how crazy boring it is to ride for more than five hours and then run for four more. What could I have been thinking? No teammates, no iPod, just lots of zero-percent body fat people who would ride over the top of me without a moment's remorse if I slid out on the sand in my next turn. I had become too accustomed to the camaraderie of a team and quickly discovered that as an adventure racing rottweiler, I had too little left in common with the poodles of the triathlon world, who live for the clock, the shaving of random body parts for the sake of speed and the glory of crossing a finish line alone. Hey, I have all the respect in the world for triathletes. They are bad asses. I was one of them for years, but that Speedo of a sport didn't suit me anymore, that's all. I had been tainted by the dirty, sweaty, leech-y, team-y Wild West of adventure racing. And so, fueled by the boredom of the endless droning of pedal strokes on the bike course, I decided to channel my inner synergist.

Within the Ironman rules, it states that there must be a three-bike-length gap between you and the person in front of you so you aren't drafting, or using the benefit of their slipstream to propel you forward. When someone passes you, you're allowed twenty seconds to re-establish that three-bike-length gap between you and the person in front of you before you're penalized. In other words, whenever some guy or girl can muster up enough energy to get past your front wheel, it's your responsibility to drop back three bike lengths. As you can imagine, this can be highly annoying for the passee, especially if the passer doesn't have the horsepower to keep that forward momentum once they get past your front wheel.

One particular guy and I seemed to be passing each other a lot, and we seemed to be going at exactly the same speed over the first twenty-five miles or so. Neither of us could get way out ahead, and it got to a point where I thought it was rather comical. I pass him, he passes me but slows down, so I pass him again. Finally, out of frustration and hearing my own voice from my presentation in my ear (imagine how annoying *that* is) saying, *Seek synergy everywhere. Create a team where there wasn't one before for mutual gain,* and, *What would a We Thinker do?* I finally sparked an idea. I realized that most of these people weren't in my division or age group, so why was I competing against them? By that same token, why in the world was everybody so wrapped up in competing with everyone else on the course?

Suddenly this seemed ludicrous to me. It was a mirror of how we react and respond to one another in our real lives: everyone against everyone. I am the only person on my team! Everyone else is someone to be passed on my way to victory! Ugh. Ewww. Because I had been reborn in the baptismal font of adventure racing, my brain was different than it was when I ran my last Ironman twelve years earlier. I had to do something about this silliness. I had to create a team in a sea of soloists. So the next time the guy passed me, I yelled out to him.

"Hey, Mike!"

"How do you know my name?" he replied.

"It's on the back of your shirt, dude!"

"Oh, yeah . . . "

He slipped into place in front of me, and I called out, "Since we're going about the same speed, do you want to play the twenty-second passing game?"

He raised his hand to let me know that he understood. What happened next was a beautiful thing. For the next eighty miles, we created a team within a solo race, completely within the "three bike lengths, twenty seconds to pass" rules. I would pass him, and he would draft right on my rear wheel for sixteen seconds and then open that three-bike-length gap with the remaining four seconds he had. Then he would pass me, and I would draft him for sixteen seconds and drop back in the final four seconds. And so on and so on.

We repeated this passing game for about three hours as we ate up the field together. Other racers couldn't imagine why in the world we were teaming up and why the heck we weren't getting caught. The race officials timed us from their motorcycles over and over again, but we were perfectly legal. And we were flying. They had never seen this crazy We Thinking behavior in an Ironman triathlon before. We were making history, and I was loving it.

Pretty soon, all the people who were yelling for the race officials to penalize us started finding like-minded people and playing the passing game, too. We had created an Iron Mutiny. We didn't change the rules that day. We just found a new way to interpret them, and we made one another a little faster by becoming teammates instead of competitors. Plus, we had a heck of a lot more fun along the way. At the end of the day, Mike and I finished with bike splits that were third and second in our respective divisions, and I had qualified for the world championships in Kona, Hawaii. It's funny how the prize in an Ironman is the invitation to another Ironman. But I was thrilled to be heading back to the big time! I guarantee it was due in major part to my friend Mike and a new vision of some old rules.

The theory of seeking synergy everywhere, even among your competitors, is this: as the finish line draws near, wouldn't you rather have a one-in-four chance of winning versus a one-in-one-hundred chance? By working together and creating that gap between you and your competitors, you're almost guaranteed to be on the podium rather than being an also-ran among the masses in the main pack. The icing on the cake is that it's a really cool feeling to collaborate for mutual gain—even if you have to sadly disappoint your new pals by beating them to the finish line!

A perfect example of We Thinking in the business world is business associations, networking events and the like, in which people from different businesses within the same industry get together for the common good of the trade. In many cases, the attendees may very well be direct competitors in certain aspects of their businesses, but the regular attendees realize that by sharing best practices and listening to the successes, failures, discoveries and opportunities uncovered by their colleagues, they make their companies and the industry as a whole stronger. I love speaking at association events and seeing people come together to network. These are generally the most successful people within their industries, which leads me to ponder whether they attend because they're successful, or if they are successful because they attend and make the most of these connections? It really is true that by helping one another, we help ourselves.

WE THINKING:
A BUSINESS CASE STUDY

When Bill Hewlett and Dave Packard founded their startup in Palo Alto, California, in 1939, they flipped a coin to decide whose name would come first on the company letterhead. Hewlett won that famous coin toss, but ultimately both men won big through the partnership that came to be known as Hewlett-Packard (HP)—all because they were two We Thinkers.

"They all worked together in that back shop behind the office, and if there was a problem, they all solved it together," said Dave's wife, Lucille. "They assumed that the other people had just as good ideas about solving problems as they did . . . I won't say I haven't seen a disagreement. Many times they've discussed the pros and cons of—and taken one side or the other of—a particular discussion. But they always came out with a compromise that seemed to satisfy both of them. I think it's a remarkable relationship."[4]

In 1958, Packard wrote "11 Simple Rules" for how he expected the HP team to behave. They are:

1. Think first of the other fellow.
2. Build up the other person's sense of importance.
3. Respect the other man's personality rights.
4. Give sincere appreciation.

---

4   http://www.hp.com/hpinfo/abouthp/histnfacts/garage/partner.html (accessed May 4, 2011).

5. Eliminate the negative.
6. Avoid openly trying to reform people.
7. Try to understand the other person.
8. Check first impressions.
9. Take care with the little details.
10. Develop genuine interest in people.
11. Keep it up.[5]

That's the perfect recipe for cooking up a We Thinking team, if you ask me. It's also the perfect recipe for a winning company: HP is the world's largest IT company, with 2010 revenues of $126 billion.

SYNERGY STARTERS: WE THINKING

Reverse Arm Wrestling

This is a fun little drill that I like to use during my presentations. I always bring it up right after I discuss the topic of We Thinking because the timing amuses me. First, I ask everyone to choose a teammate, and then I describe the game like this: "This game is called reverse arm wrestling, and here's how it's played. Your goal *and your teammate's goal* is to get your own arm down to the table as many times as you can in thirty seconds. So instead of pushing your teammate's arm down, as is the case with standard arm wrestling, your mutual goal is to get your own arm down to the table. *Capisce?* Ready, set, go!"

---

5   Hewlett-Packard, "HP Timeline," http://www8.hp.com/us/en/hp-information/about-hp/history/hp-timeline/hp-timeline.html (accessed May 4, 2011).

It's always interesting to see how many people have a death grip on each another, struggling to not let the other person get his or her own arm down to the table versus the number of pairs that embrace the We Thinking concept and instantly cooperate and go back and forth to both sides as quickly as they can. At the end of the thirty seconds, I ask people to raise their hands if they got their own arm down to the table five times or less. It's generally between twenty and forty percent of the room. Then I ask how many people got their own arm down to the table twenty times or more. The We Thinkers of the group, usually about twenty percent of the room, proudly raise their hands.

I ask them if they just missed breakfast this morning or if they need to start lifting weights—or if perhaps there was a method to their madness. Then I have one of the We Thinkers stand up and explain what their team did. Invariably, they will say something to the effect of, "Well, you said this was my teammate, so we just worked together!" That comment is usually followed by a collective groan from the people in the room who almost blew an artery trying to keep their "teammate" from succeeding.

Then I pose the question, "Isn't it better for both of you to look at each another, realize you have the same goal and help each other get thirty, rather than compete against each other and have both of you get zero?"

It's a fun, upbeat drill, but with a deep and meaningful point: Why are we as human beings so wired to see winning as being mutually exclusive, a solo endeavor? Why do we constantly think that in order for us to win, someone else always has to lose? A true We Thinker sees a world full of teammates versus a world full of competitors. When I say your goal and your teammate's goal is to get as many as you can, what makes us unable to overcome that competitive drive, even among our own teammates? Granted, I believe that competition is healthy and that it's infused into our DNA through our many successful solo endeavors in school, sports, climbing the corporate ladder and so on. But the most enlightened We Thinkers understand that their competitors are not the people in their family, within their community or within their own company, which is where we tend to compete most often. So we have to ask ourselves, who is on our team? Are we competing when we could be creating synergy instead?

If you're standing there all alone on the playing field of life every day, you have a little bit of We Thinking to do!

The Lost Keys

Here's another little gem of a We Thinking test that I learned about back when I was in college. It was how several of my girlfriends tested their dates to see if they were good boyfriend material, but as a leader, you can use it to find out if a job candidate or a new hire is a We Thinking person.

At the end of the job interview or team meeting, suddenly stop and say, "Oh no! I've lost my keys! I know I just had them right here. Now where could they be?" As you start looking around for your pretend lost keys, note the response from the other person or people in the room. Some will just sit there as if to say, "Bummer, I hope you find them soon," or even go to the next step and ask, "Where did you last see them?" But the biggest We Thinker in the room will jump up and start looking around the house or office with you, making your problem their problem. It's a simple but effective way to discover a person's potential as a teammate.

ELEMENT 6:

OWNERSHIP OF THE PROJECT

"To promote cooperation and teamwork, remember:
People tend to resist that which is forced upon them.
People tend to support that which they help create."

—Vince Pfaff

Ever feel like you're dragging your teammates along toward your goal and not theirs? How do you get and keep your teammates on board for the long haul, focused and driven to succeed? The truth is that ownership comes from inspiration, and inspiration is an inside job. As a leader, you can help facilitate inspiration, but you can't necessarily create it. I believe that a team can create short-term motivation by using rewards like a cruise or a cash bonus for certain measurable behaviors. But long-term inspiration comes only from the heart and mind of the inspired.

People who are inspired by a project will own it. They will have an entrepreneurial drive associated with the goal that can't be bought with money. And they will wring themselves out to make it happen. A leader's dream team.

"MOTIVATION IS FOR NOW; INSPIRATION IS FOREVER."

So how do we inspire our teammates to drive hard for months or even years toward a common goal? The key is in making the desired outcome their goal, too, not just a company goal or a target passed down from the leadership cloud. This is accomplished in one of two ways: hiring the inspired and inspiring the hired.

HIRE THE INSPIRED

There's a lot to be said for hiring well. Often we are given an employee or teammate who is competent in a particular technical area of the business, which is the reason they were hired, but somehow they are missing that inspiration chip in their psyche that's necessary to own outcomes and get to the finish line at all costs. I'm of the opinion that when there is a job that can be taught and learned, we're better off being guided in our teammate selection by their inspiration to succeed against all odds versus strictly their technical competence (unless we're talking about surgery, nuclear fission, NASA engineers or something of the same ilk, granted).

For example, I've watched many a world-champion mountain biker, kayak paddler, runner or triathlete pull the plug on their adventure racing team the moment they found themselves outside their comfort zone, felt that their environment was beyond their control or when they believed they were suffering too much relative to past experiences. When times got tough, they quit.

I've also witnessed true competitors who were slightly above-average athletes who ended up on the podium because there was no challenge they couldn't overcome with their team. They were willing to do whatever it took because getting to that finish line was a goal that lay deep within their souls. They would learn, be, adapt to, evolve into whatever they needed to complete the job and not let their teammates down. I would take an inspired person over a competent one any day of the week. Obviously, the best-case scenario is to find a person with both inspiration and competence.

A great leader will find out what their team members are truly inspired to do when there is a lack of external motivation. Who are they at their core? What are they drawn to in their everyday lives? Are they social or introverted? Are they involved with kids, charities, sports? Do they most often mention dollars, recognition or personal achievement when they talk about what they hope to get out of their jobs? What subjects cause them to light up when they're talking about them? That is the source of their inspiration, and that's really good to know. If you can somehow tie your outcomes and goals to the source of your teammate's inspiration, you're golden.

All too often, we try to motivate our teammates with a set reward system, but inspiration is not a one-size-fits-all proposition. Think about how you motivate your kids. We all know what inspires our kids because we study them intensely from the time they are born. We know how to help them achieve their dreams. Why not do the same with the adults around us? We will not only create lifelong bonds but also create world-class teammates who will succeed against all odds.

Take Starbucks, for example. In the early days of my career as a speaker and team builder, I did a number of events for this company. Immediately after one of my first keynote speeches, a vice president approached me and asked if I had ever worked for Starbucks or studied their employee handbook because my message about creating human connections and inspiring team members was eerily similar to their company philosophy.

He went on to explain that Starbucks's success was not a result of its stores brewing excellent coffee. It was about "creating exceptional experiences" for their guests. According to the company philosophy, every Starbucks should have just the right smell, lighting, temperature and layout. Guests should be greeted by happy, smiling baristas and team members who know their names, know their favorite drinks and make them feel like family. In other words, the coffee is incidental to the experience of being inside a Starbucks. It's that experience that makes us want to come back again and again. And we do.

The Starbucks vice president explained that his company realized that the business of coffee can be learned, but far more important to them in the hiring process is that their store managers are *inspired to create exceptional experiences for people*. In fact, several of their interview questions revolved around asking the prospective manager about times when they created meaningful experiences for their friends, family and classmates, and how and why they did it. At the core of these questions was detecting an existing inspiration to be an exceptional host to hundreds of guests every day. The burning desire to be hospitable and nurturing comes from a human place in one's soul, not from an employee manual. The business of coffee can be learned, but hiring inspired people who are passionate about providing exceptional experiences for their customers is what made Starbucks a global coffee dynasty.

INSPIRE THE HIRED

If people don't come to us ready-made with that "inspiration chip" to embrace the goals of the team, or if they seem to be losing owner-ship along the way, there are ways to create that spark inside them again. It all comes down to remembering this chapter's opening quote: "People tend to resist that which is forced upon them. People tend to embrace that which they help create." The goal is to reinvig-orate the entrepreneurial spirit in each of our teammates by giving them the sense that the outcome is truly up to them and reminding them that they're uniquely qualified to be key players in the team's success. How?

Discover and Fulfill Core Needs

Great leaders and teammates have a keen insight into what makes each of their teammates tick or come alive. They know what their teammates are inspired by, what they pride themselves on and what they need in order to be motivated. Not everyone is inspired by a big-ger paycheck. Some people are more inspired by recognition, specific rewards, a heartfelt thank-you from the powers that be, or the oppor-tunity for advancement or to move into a job that uniquely matches their talents. If we discover our teammates' core needs, we have the key to inspiring them by finding a way to help them fulfill those needs. For example, as the CEO of The Project Athena Foundation, I study every one of the people I bring on board to find the best fit for them within the organization based on who they are at their core instead of hiring them for a specific job description. The *person* is hired first; the job they eventually do longer term is based on their natural tendencies, passion and interests. The caring connectors end up working with our Survivors to coach them and facilitate their success. The entrepreneurial thinkers and natural spokespeople become our PR and marketing outreach specialists, and the process-oriented work as race and event planners. I also make sure that their "bonuses" are customized based on their specific needs and life goals. For some it's a cash bonus, for another, a free trip to hike across the Grand Canyon with our Survivors, and for another, a training package and entry fee to a triathlon. Obviously, this is much simpler in a small company, but even in a larger one, you can create special awards and ways to recognize people that will make them feel that you "see" them and value their individual contributions. When people feel that they are "special" to the people they respect and love, there is no stopping them on their mission!

Employ a Democratic Leadership Style

Nothing inspires an entrepreneurial spirit like being asked for one's input and opinion. With a democratic and inclusive leadership style, you can move a teammate from being part of the audience to becoming a proactive and instrumental part of the solution in minutes. It's amazing how often we make the mistake of handing someone "their goals" from

"PEOPLE WILL EMBRACE THAT WHICH THEY HELP CREATE."

on high without asking for their input or getting their buy-in on what's possible from their perspective.

Back in my pharmaceutical sales days, there was an annual goal handed down for me to meet each year, which I'm pretty certain was one tenth of our district goal because there were ten of us in the field. I did the best I could, and I did well, but I certainly wasn't inspired. Looking back, they would have gotten so much more out of me had they asked me what my challenges were in that particular district, or in which local hospital systems my drugs were on formulary and how they might help me expand reach, or where we were suffering as a brand, or where we were losing business and why, or even what I thought my district was capable of in terms of market share. It seemed to me that the company was telling me that my business goals were really none of my business. Motivating? Inspiring? Not.

The best teammates and leaders realize that we all want to feel like we have contributed to the success of an organization, a family, a relationship; and a key way to inspire that entrepreneurial spirit is to listen to our teammates, hear their opinions and solicit their ideas. Nothing shows a teammate that they are respected and valued more than seeing their ideas and comments acted on and incorporated by the team. People will embrace that which they help create.

Value Unique Competencies

Everyone has or knows something valuable that they can contribute to the team, whether it's life experience, education, specific knowledge, a keen sense of the market or a magic way with people. The best teams discover and mine those talents for the good of the team without being hamstrung by rank, seniority, tenure or titles. If you instill in your corporate culture that even the newest people on your team are recognized and valued for their strengths and are given a platform to share those strengths with the team, you will have a truly inspired employee.

For example, on our all-female fire crew (yeah, sistahs!), Dana, our captain, brings the sense of friendship and a "people first" mentality, and she is known for being straightforward and making great decisions. She is also the leader who is always on the side of her crew. In the corporate arena of "us" versus "them," she is always "us." We tell her how glad we are to have her as our captain and leader every day. Melissa brings the heart and an amazing mechanical ability. She is 5'9" and 130 pounds (tiny but mighty!) and drives the fire engine like a champ. She is also our go-to person when the you know what hits the fan. She always assures us that everything is going to be okay. And we believe her. April is our paramedic and the authority on all things medical. She's the class clown and keeps us in stitches most of the day. I'm the grunt firefighter and EMT. I'm valued for creating fun workouts and being good with patients—but *not* for my cooking.

In a paramilitary organization like the fire department, it would be easy to have a top-down leadership style, with one person barking orders and taking the credit, and the other three people running around and doing their bidding. But our crew breaks the mold not only for our gender but also because we are a world-class team in every sense of the word. After working together for years, we don't see rank. We see collections of valued competencies, and we recognize and count on those key strengths in one another. It's inspiring to work on a team that "sees" you and loves you for who you are and what you bring to the team and the community. It really feels like we can do just about anything together, and I can't wait to get to work each day.

When I was a substitute teacher for a couple of years between my sales and firefighting jobs, I had to figure out some new ways to forge inspiration in physical education class. Right off the bat, I noticed that kids today don't really like running as much as I did when I was that age. But I also noticed that the other coaches had made running into a chore, with punishment as a consequence.

"Okay, guys, you know the drill," the coaches barked at their disengaged students. "Everybody walks or runs the mile, or you're staying after school. Let's go."

On my first day at one particular middle school, I watched as the usual protocol unfolded. Five to ten kids ran, another ten to fifteen walked and pushed each other and goofed off, and a gaggle of girls sat on the bleachers and looked at their makeup and fixed their hair. What the heck? School had changed a lot since I was a kid. Why did these students have no desire to be great or to even be good or to even care? I had to find out if it was circumstance or a whole new generation of slackers.

So the next day, I came up with a plan. Instead of telling them they had to run a mile, I decided to gather them on the bleachers and ask them how many of them thought they were strong enough to run a mile. About seventy percent of the class raised a hand. Then I asked them who thought they could run it in under eight minutes. I brought out a bag of Charms Blow Pops and a bag of quarters, and I told them that anyone who ran or walked the mile in under twelve minutes would get a blow pop, and anyone who ran it in eight or less would get a blow pop and a quarter. Lo and behold, the benches cleared, and the kids scrambled to the starting line (with the exception of a trio of "too cool for school" girls and a couple of kids on the injured reserve list).

As the other kids assembled on the track, I walked over to the group of makeup-and-hair girls and asked them if they had any ideas on how they could motivate the kids out there who needed their help. Did any of them know any cheers or anything? Without waiting for an answer, I walked to the track, hoping for the best. When I said go, half of the class took off like they were shot out of a cannon. The rest started at a steady run in little groups, just hoping to finish in less than twelve minutes. I stood there marveling at how easy it was to go from fifty percent buy-in the day before to ninety percent buy-in by just asking these kids if they thought they could do it instead of forcing them to, and providing a few pennies' worth of positive reinforcement.

At the end of the third lap, a cheer even rose up from the makeup girls in the stands for the boy who was leading the race. Even they had realized that the "cool people" were now on the field instead of in the stands, and they were inspired to be a part of it, too. Everyone got a blow pop that day, and I gave away twelve quarters. It was a cheap price to pay for showing kids how much they're really capable of when they actually try. Each day after that became a different fun event, such as giving the girls a one-minute lead and seeing how many boys could catch them, giving awards for any boy who could run the mile under six minutes and any girl under seven minutes, giving awards for "best cheerleading squad" among the kids who were injured on the sidelines, and giving "most consistent" and "most inspirational runner" awards at the end of the week so that the kids who weren't the fastest but who showed the most heart also had their moment in the sun.

Before I knew it, we had full participation and one hundred percent buy-in. And it didn't take much, aside from fulfilling the kids' core needs for recognition, money and candy, and allowing them the grace to rise to the occasion of their own volition. I didn't *make* them run. I *motivated and inspired* them to run, or at the very least, to participate within their strengths and capabilities. It was all up to them, and they proved me right for believing in them beyond reason. These kids learned how amazing they were in the weeks that I was there. They learned that fitness is cool, and I sincerely hope that they were inspired to continue using the tools they discovered they had to go beyond what they believed was possible. As you can see, it certainly didn't take much, just a little bit of creativity and some positive reinforcement.

If you give a person a say in their own goals, ask them what they can do and give them the grace to rise as high as they choose, value and applaud their unique competencies and strengths, and help them fulfill core needs, you will have an inspired teammate for life.

We do these motivational kinds of things for our children a lot, don't we? Then why do we so rarely make similar attempts to inspire our family members, our coworkers and our teammates? Are we being shy as leaders or thinking that it's not really our place? Remember, there's still a kid inside of each of us, a kid who wants recognition and to feel special around the people they admire. You'll be pleasantly surprised at how far a little bit of positive feedback will go. Sometimes it only takes a lollipop and a quarter to inspire greatness.

****

So let's take a look at the magic that happens when you as a leader are able to blend hiring the inspired with inspiring the hired. A Borneo villager named Dawat Mutang and the French Team Intersport are an unlikely but perfect example of the heights you can achieve when you get it *just* right.

For the 1994 Raid Gauloises, the race organizers dragged us deep into one of the most remote parts of Borneo. It took us three days just to get to the starting line, a little jungle village with six huts and a tiny schoolhouse in which we were all supposed to sleep the night before the big race. Getting to the village was like a re-run of the movie *Planes, Trains and Automobiles*. When we finally arrived, I remember walking around the huts thinking how insulated these people were. There was no need for cars or any form of transportation. If you wanted to find a wife or husband, you'd just walk over to the next village and get one. Totally isolated from the outside world, this village and its immediate surroundings were all these people had ever known, or ever would know.

On day one of the race, as we were all lining up for the morning start, a member of the French team was walking toward the starting line and broke his ankle. Click. Broke. Done. Four people had to start and finish the race, or the entire team would be disqualified, so Team Intersport had a decision to make: do we start the race with three people, take the ensuing disqualification and just go on an adventure, or do we try to find a way to make this work so we can at least start the race with a full team? They decided that it was better to try and fail than to never try at all. So they quickly started knocking on the doors of the village's makeshift huts looking for someone to replace their injured teammate, and Dawat Mutang opened one of those doors. Dawat, a thirty-five-year-old farmer and father of three, did not speak a word of French, and the French team didn't speak English. So Team Intersport stood on Dawat's stoop, trying to explain adventure racing to him and sizing him up for the Lycra team outfit. After quickly discussing with his wife the idea of going on this crazy adventure with people he had never seen to places he had never been doing things he'd never done, Dawat shrugged his shoulders, smiled and said to the cameras as he walked toward the starting line, "I don't know exactly what is going to happen, but I'm confident I can work it with a team."

And that's how Dawat Mutang became an international adventure racing sensation. Team Intersport threw some Lycra team tights on him, gave him all of the injured teammate's equipment and started the race. So what if he had never paddled a canoe or been inside a cave or used climbing gear or rappelled or even ridden a bike (can you believe it?)—all of which would be required to complete the race.

Dawat was the weakest link when it came to the technical aspects of adventure racing, but it turns out that he had the attitude and spirit of a winner. Team Intersport had not only Hired the Inspired, but they also Inspired the Hired by letting Dawat lead wherever he was strongest or had valuable local information. He knew how to deal with the different kinds of mud they encountered, the varied terrain and how to bushwhack effectively from village to village. Team Intersport didn't just drag Dawat along with them; they put him right out front from the beginning. For four days, they ran, shot rapids, pedaled, climbed, rappelled and caved their way across Borneo, with good-natured Dawat right alongside them for the entire grueling trip, learning as he went. Although it was his first time on a bike, Dawat never made any excuses, even when he flew over the handlebars on a big downhill run. In an interview after the crash, Dawat said with a smile, "Oh yes, I have fallen once, but it was my fault because they had shown me how to handle the brakes. So I used the front brake instead of the rear one, and it just kicked me out from the pedals!"

"IT'S NOT NECESSARILY WHAT YOU KNOW THAT MAKES YOU A GREAT TEAMMATE BUT WHAT YOU'RE WILLING TO LEARN."

Talk about personal ownership.

Miraculously, Team Intersport finished second overall, only four hours behind the first-place team. When his cheering teammates hoisted him onto their shoulders at the end of the race, a joyous Dawat toasted them with bottled water and ceremoniously poured some over their heads in celebration. And the crowd went wild. Everyone cheered Dawat, not because he and his team came in second but because he had been willing to step outside of the familiarity of his daily life and try something entirely new and completely foreign to him—and the team had succeeded beyond their wildest dreams.

"So many things to learn. Really fantastic," a grinning Dawat told a television reporter afterward. "When I get back home, probably if I tell it to my village, the people won't believe it. Something so fantastic . . . I won't forget this."

Dawat teaches us that it's not necessarily what you know that makes you a great teammate but what you're willing to learn, and how enthusiastically you embrace the project's end goals. In many cases, you can learn as you go, or as I often say, you can jump off that cliff and grow your wings on the way down. It's not always about coming to the table as the smartest guy in the room. Being a successful teammate means trusting and embracing your team and its goal, and having the type of ownership that says, *no matter what comes along, I can handle it with these guys.* When Dawat said yes to Team Intersport, he took ownership of that race. He cared as much about it as his veteran teammates did, and together they accomplished an amazing thing. Perhaps Team Intersport could have found a more experienced athlete than Dawat, but they could not have picked a better, more inspired teammate. As it turned out, that was the key to their success.

OWNERSHIP OF THE PROJECT:
A BUSINESS CASE STUDY

One of the best corporate examples of project ownership is Southwest Airlines. Founded in Texas in 1971 with only three airplanes, Southwest was decidedly different from day one—its focus was on providing both its customers *and* its employees with an exceptional experience. According to Southwest's website, the company mission statement not only promises to treat each of its customers with reverence...

> *[Our mission] is dedication to the highest quality of customer service delivered with a sense of warmth, friendliness, individual pride and company spirit.*

...but also its employees:

We are committed to provide our employees a stable work environment with equal opportunity for learning and personal growth. Creativity and innovation are encouraged for improving the effectiveness of Southwest Airlines. Above all, employees will be provided the same concern, respect and caring attitude within the organization that they are expected to share externally with every Southwest customer.

Southwest CEO Gary Kelly clearly strives to hire the inspired and inspire his hires. "Southwest is a company of people, not just planes. We hire great people who have a passion for serving others, and we give them the freedom to be themselves and to take care of our customers. We treat our employees like family," he said.[6]

The list of Southwest employee perks is long. Profit-sharing, free travel for employees and their families, discounts for theme parks, rental cars and hotels, dollar-for-dollar match on the 401k, a discount on stock purchases, health insurance plans starting at $15 per month, extensive ongoing training, an in-house promotion policy and lots of fun parties are only a few of the benefits Southwest's employees enjoy. But despite the focus on generosity and lighthearted fun, the company still manages to get the job done right, earning

6   Alan C. Greenberg, *Memos from the Chairman* (New York: Workman, 1996).

multiple awards year after year for its customer service, on-time flights and easy check-in experience. Oh, and did I mention that Southwest has been profitable for thirty-eight years in a row?

Apparently, giving people ownership of a company really *does* make good business sense.

SYNERGY STARTERS: OWNERSHIP OF THE PROJECT

To discover team members' inspiration, how they would like to be viewed and the key to their motivation:

This is an easy one…people love to answer these kinds of questions, and it really demonstrates how much the company cares about them as human beings and not just employees, so just ask! Stress that honesty is the key (and that they should not respond with what they think is "the right answer"). Hand your team members a questionnaire with the following questions:

1. What would your job/mission be if money was no object?
2. What motivates you to do your best and meet your goals?
3. What is your favorite part of your job?
4. What do you wish you could do more of/less of when it comes to your daily work responsibilities?
5. When you retire, what is it that you would like people to be inspired to say about you?

6. What would you like to be best known and remembered for?

A leader armed with this information is in a perfect position to create "buy in" from their teammates by gaining new insight into what motivates them, what inspires them and how they see themselves and their contributions. If you can give your teammates more of what inspires them in their daily work lives, and recognize them for the contributions that are most important to them, you'll have very engaged and energized team members.

ELEMENT 7:

RELINQUISHMENT OF EGO

"Strategically placed testosterone never put out a fire."
—Chief Alan Brunacini, Phoenix Fire Department

Okay, gang, it's time to take a look at the easiest but scariest essential element! Most people would rather relinquish their credit cards than their ego. And I totally understand. You're probably thinking that having an intact, healthy ego is what got you here, at the top of your game, surrounded by people who think you're pretty smart and capable and talented. You would never have had the courage to do half the things you've done in your life without your ego intact, right? So what's this talk about relinquishing it?

Let's start the discussion by looking at the difference between confidence and ego because I think that quite often we get the two confused. Confidence is the better looking, smarter fraternal twin of ego. Confidence is strength of character based on life experience and continued success, whereas ego is a weakness of character, based on insecurity and fear. The world's best teammates always bring their confidence to the mission but understand that their egos are going to be the heaviest things in their packs. It's time to lighten the load.

LEAVE YOUR EGO AT THE STARTING LINE

Sometimes, the best way to propel your team to the finish line is by leaving your ego at the starting line. At the 2006 Primal Quest in Utah, the organizers gave every team one horse for the first leg, with the rule that we could carry up to 250 pounds on horseback and not an ounce more. That was really nice of them because right at the start there was a grueling sixty-five-mile jeep trail run followed by another thirty-five-mile off-road hike and run through the desert. Under those circumstances, a horse is a good thing to have. So they handed over the reins, and all the other teams started putting their packs on their horse, preparing to run alongside their loyal steed for the next sixty-five miles.

Now, it was common knowledge on my teams that during the first couple of days of a race, when all hell was breaking loose, I was usually the person who was struggling to keep up. It's just a physiological fact that women generally can't run as fast as the top men in the sport because of the difference in oxygen-carrying capacity and anaerobic threshold. Especially if they are, as my sister and I like to call it, "not frail" like me. However, I would come into my own by day three or four and sometimes even get stronger as time went on. I was clearly more of an endgame player.

"CONFIDENCE IS STRENGTH OF CHARACTER BASED ON LIFE EXPERIENCE AND CONTINUED SUCCESS."

In this particular race, my teammates really wanted to go hard and stay out front from the beginning. I was the captain of Team Merrell/Zanfel, a pack of elite New Zealand multisport athletes who were in it to win it, as was I. We all knew I wasn't going to be able to keep up with them at the front of the race on a one-hundred-mile run. I would have tried my best, to be sure, but I would have been trashed by the end of the first leg.

So my teammates came up with a solution. Instead of just using the horse to carry all of our packs, they would put two packs and *me* on the horse, and I would ride while they ran that first sixty-five-mile trail run, saving my strength for the thirty-five-mile off-road desert trek and beyond.

I was mortified, to put it mildly, because several of the other top women were running, but after thinking about it for a minute or two, I knew they were right. Having me ride was our best chance at the overall win.

So I left my ego and my Superwoman cape at the starting line and got on that silly horse. I have never been so embarrassed in my entire life. There I was, trotting down the jeep trail like I was in an old Western movie, while everyone from the top-five teams—including all the other women—ran alongside me and Old Paint.

****

"How's the view up there, John Wayne?" one of my competitors threw out as a good-natured jab as she ran by, smiling.

"Having a good time, Queen of Sheba?" asked one of the race crew members at the first water stop.

Ugh. I had to relinquish my ego entirely in order to resist the urge to crawl under a rock. I kept telling myself that my team and I would have the last laugh, that my confidence in the decision was warranted and that this moment of humiliation was going to pay off eventually. And it did. After we gave up the horses, there was still the off-road desert hike and run left, which I blazed through in style, taking care of my teammates and keeping them fed and hydrated along the way. That set us up for success over the next six days of nonstop racing, while many of the other teams were in survival mode after that first leg. For over six hundred miles of mountain biking, hiking, kayaking and rope work, I was able to hold my own and not only keep up with the guys but also carry extra weight in the closing hours, which we desperately needed in a last-minute struggle for third place against the Canadian team. *We just* edged them out at the finish line, literally running neck and neck on day six. If I had run that first sixty-five miles at my maximum pace, this story would have had a completely different ending.

My teammates and I were only protecting our assets and thinking about our long-term success by having me ride that first leg instead of run. Before the race started, the other teams batted around the idea of having someone ride their horses, but nobody would swallow their pride and do it. I agreed to do it because that was what it was going to take for our team to finish strong and at the front of the pack. I'm convinced that leaving my ego at the starting line was what got us onto the podium. The way I see it, a podium finish lasts forever—and it was the perfect bandage for my momentarily bruised ego.

IT'S OKAY TO ASK FOR HELP

It's often hard for those of us with a healthy ego to accept help from other people. We see that as a sign of weakness. But accepting help from your teammates is vital to the building of your team, so from now on I want you to think differently about accepting help. I want you to think about accepting help as giving a gift to the helper. When you accept help from someone else, it makes the other person feel worthy. It makes them feel important; it makes them feel liked. If it's hard for you to accept help for help's sake, try thinking of it as giving a gift to the helper. For example, think of how great it makes you feel when you are able to open a door for someone who is struggling with a handful of groceries or battling with a set of crutches. It makes your heart expand a little, doesn't it? You feel great about yourself. You feel connected to that person; you feel a positive vibe and a bond.

Don't pass up those kinds of opportunities when it comes to your team. People are already going out on a limb to ask you if you need help, so accept it. Every time. Whether you need it or not. Find a reason to say yes and give that person the gift of accepting the help. It's a great team building tool that is vastly underutilized.

> **"ACCEPTING HELP IS A GIFT TO THE HELPER."**

Conversely, asking for help is also a gift to the helper. Being asked for help makes people feel needed and strong, and it most definitely makes them step up their game when they get the chance to be the hero.

It was by happy accident that I discovered the power of this concept in the Patagonia Expedition Race in 2004. It was the first time that our newest teammate, New Zealander Chris Morrissey, had ever raced with a top-ranked team, and because he was a superstar short course racer, he was struggling by day four. So I decided to apply a bit of psychological strategy to see if I could get him back into the game. Heck, I was suffering, too, so it was worth a shot. On the hiking leg, I asked him if he could throw me his towline because my blisters were slowing me down and I needed some help. As soon as I asked for that towline, I saw a startling difference in Chris. Suddenly he went from being a guy who was worried and struggling and suffering to someone who was practically on fire. He turned into a world-class racer right before my eyes, and all it took was me asking him to give me a hand. It was similar to what Robert Nagle did for me in Ecuador when the time came for me to climb that volcano, when he put his hand on my shoulder and told me that my team was counting on me, that they needed my help.

I guess it's wired into the human DNA to rise to the occasion when somebody needs help. Because that's a universal truth, I wonder why we so often refuse help when it's offered to us or fail to ask when we need it. When you refuse help, you're missing an opportunity to connect to another person. When you help others, you like them, they like you, and you feel the power of unity. Don't let your ego get in the way of making those kinds of connections. Relinquish your ego and ask for help. Accept help. Give that gift. Allow a teammate the chance to step up to the plate (even if you don't necessarily need it) and watch them shine. It inspires and motivates everyone involved.

VALUE TEAM SUCCESS OVER INDIVIDUAL GLORY

In 2001, I was invited to race the New Zealand Eco-Challenge with Team EarthLink, a great group of guys who knew a thing or two about valuing team success over individual glory. One of them was Roman Dial, a hard-core outdoorsman from Alaska who is a ten-time winner of the Alaska Mountain Wilderness Classic ten-day multisport race, and also a scientist and college professor. Roman told us at the start that he hadn't done a lot of training for this race; in fact, he admitted that he had "kind of just hopped off the couch." But Roman was a fierce competitor and a world-class teammate who was willing to relinquish his ego for the good of the team. So too was our team captain, Jason Middleton, a top triathlete who was a very good adventure racer but new to the sheer speed of racing at the front of the pack. With some pretty solid experience in what it takes to win big international races under our belts, my third teammate, Isaac Wilson, and I started pushing the pace early, hoping to remain within striking distance of the leaders.

On the first major mountain climb, Isaac and I started to drop Roman and Jason. Suddenly I realized that I was finally in a position to help the guys on my team! Yes! But although I felt that I had enough strength at that moment to carry some of their gear, I was a bit hesitant to make the offer because you never know how people are going to react. Out of sheer desperation from watching the other top teams disappear over the peak, I finally got up the nerve to approach Jason and ask if I could take some of the heavier equipment out of his pack. And bless his heart, he said, "Hell, yeah! By all means!" I was so excited and thrilled to finally be the person who could help versus the person being helped. We stopped, quickly transferred some of his heavier gear into my pack and suffered equally all the way to the peak, where we were once again in sight of the leaders.

Later in the race, Roman was suffering on another vertical climb. I was behind him trying to encourage and push him verbally, when I wondered what would happen if I physically pushed him. In past races, teammates had pushed me (gently, of course) up some hills when I was beginning to lag, and it had helped me immensely. So I took a deep breath, reached up under Roman's pack and pushed him on the small of his back to propel him up the mountain. I almost expected him to say, "Hey! Get off me!" but instead he said, "Awesome! Thanks, Rob!" Sweet! That was music to my ears. What a thrill it was to be the pusher instead of the pushee. Roman and I created a pretty cool bond on the daylong climb up that peak, a bond that was a benefit to our team and our souls. And we all enjoyed the excitement of keeping up with the front runners by creating synergy.

"HEROISM ELEVATES SOMEONE; HUMILITY ELEVATES EVERYONE."

Looking back, it amazes me that both Jason and Roman let me help them. But what makes it doubly amazing is that there was a television crew from the Discovery Channel filming the entire thing. Jason and Roman valued our team's success over their individual glory so much that they allowed the entire world to watch them receiving help from a girl.

In our post-race interview, Roman said, "I had no pride. My pride was in the team, you know? So I just let her do it," to which he added with a smile, "Have you seen her? Her arms are bigger than mine! That's a strong woman."

How can you not love that guy? Quirky? Way. Great team-mate? Definitely.

We finished that race in fourth place, and even though we didn't have the physical fire power to make the podium, I adored my teammates because they accepted my help for the good of the team. And I felt so great about being a contributing team member throughout the race that I had one of the best race experiences of my life. No wonder the guys on my other teams always wanted to help me; it's the best feeling in the world to alleviate someone else's suffering and, in the process, get to the finish line faster.

LEAD FROM THE BACK OF THE PACK

Often, we leaders believe that we need to be out front leading the charge in order to be effective.

"Hey, everybody, over here!" we seem to say. "Do it just like me! Notice me, victoriously leading by example!"

But now I know that the best leaders are the ones who stand back and lead from behind. They marshal their people as if they're a flock of sheep by hanging back and making sure that everything is going well, by ensuring that everyone has the tools they need to be successful. Great leaders ensure that their teammates are given the opportunity to amaze and inspire themselves every day, rather than being led by a pacesetter who will never allow himself to be caught.

As you move through your day, think about leading from the back of the pack instead of always being in the front. You can't see the rest of your team if you're out front, can you? But you can see and guide everybody toward greatness if you're behind them, literally and figuratively.

GIVE AWAY THE CREDIT

My teammate Keith Murray showed me the power and grace of giving away the credit in a remarkable way in the Tibet–Nepal Raid Gauloises. You remember Keith, the one who said that people will remember you not by what you do but what your attitude is for things. Not only could he pull inspirational quotes out of thin air at the most opportune moments, but he was also the strongest guy on the team, the biggest stud.

So it was no surprise when Keith volunteered to carry my pack at the beginning of the race. We started that race at 14,000 feet, and he had the greatest oxygen-carrying capacity on the team. At that point in my racing career, I rarely turned down help at the start of a race because that's where I suffered the most. So Keith took my pack and put it on top of his. He didn't just take out a few heavy items, mind you. No, he put my entire thirty-pound pack on top of his forty-five-pound pack and carried them both up and over seemingly every peak in the Himalayas for three nonstop days and nights. The load Keith carried stretched from below his butt to over the top of his head. And not only was he carrying a ridiculous amount of weight in a harsh, oxygen-free environment during an ultra endurance feat beyond human comprehension, but also he was running ahead to the next lake or river with all of our CamelBak bladders hanging off him like octopus tentacles and filling them for us so we would never have to stop moving forward or take a break. He was like the Tasmanian Devil out there.

But here's the most amazing thing: as we approached the transition area at the end of those first three days, we could see off in the distance that there were television cameras there waiting to document our arrival. As soon as Keith saw those cameras, when they were still far out of range, he took my pack off, sat it on the ground next to him and continued walking so that I could come up behind him, put my pack on and head into the transition area with my dignity intact. Not a word was spoken; there was not even a backward glance. Just this silent grace.

Most guys would have come into the transition area thrilled that they were going to get some camera time to document their studliness. But not Keith. He didn't need it, didn't want it. It was not important to him to get the credit for carrying my pack for three days. What was important to him? The team. That we looked strong and that I felt good about myself. That there wasn't any whispering among the other teams about our having a weak link and being vulnerable. Keith didn't need the rest of the world to know he was a superstar. His teammates knew it, and that was all that mattered to him. I loved him so much for that, for giving away the credit. It's something I will never forget.

RELINQUISHMENT OF EGO:
A BUSINESS CASE STUDY

In a 2009 study by the University of Southern California's Marshall School of Business and Stanford University,[7] researchers conducted multiple experiments to uncover the effect that ego protection has on groups. Unsurprising, the effects were damaging. The researchers found that when leaders try to deflect blame for their mistakes or otherwise preserve their self-image, then the leaders, their organizations, their people and society all suffer.

"When we see others protecting their egos, we become defensive too," said Professor Nathanael J. Fast, the study's lead author. "We then try to protect our own self-image by blaming others for our mistakes, which may feel good in the moment...[but] blame creates a culture of fear, and this leads to a host of negative consequences for individuals and for groups."[8]

In other words, Fast and his fellow researcher, Larissa Tiedens, found that when leaders try to protect their egos, that kind of behavior goes viral. One experiment showed that when people saw one person wrongly blame another, they were more likely to repeat that sort of face-saving behavior themselves.

---

7   Nathanael J. Fast and Larissa Z. Tiedens, "Blame Contagion: The Automatic Transmission of Self-Serving Attributions," *Journal of Experimental Social Psychology* 46 (2010): 97–106.

8   Karen Lowe, "People Like to Play the Blame Game," *USC News,* November 24, 2009, http://uscnews.usc.edu/business/people_like_to_play_the_blame_game.html (accessed June 4, 2011).

To foster a positive business culture and healthy human relations, the researchers suggest that managers set their egos aside and humbly admit their errors publicly, and also create an environment in which their people are actually rewarded for learning from their mistakes. The researchers also recommend that whenever it's necessary to discuss a subordinate's misstep, the conversation should be between the manager and the subordinate only, and kept totally private.

SYNERGY STARTERS: **RELINQUISHMENT OF EGO**

To get your team to acknowledge the accomplishments of others (and keep their confidence intact, too):

- During a long-term project or lull in motivation, get your team together for a quick "Gold Star" lunch/celebration in which employees award *one another* (it's nice when it's from within the team and not from upper management) a symbolic "Gold Star" for their contributions, attitude, teamwork, whatever their team members think is great about their efforts. These gold stars can be in the form of a grab bag of prizes, restaurant gift certificates and so on. The session should be free flowing, with employees coming to the front of the room, making an announcement about another employee, giving that person an award and moving to the next announcement until everyone is done. This is a great way to create a positive environment in which employees see how good it feels to "give away the credit" and be gracious about acknowledging the contributions of the people around them. It also helps employees realize that if they don't try to "grab" credit for themselves all the time, others are far more motivated to "give" it to them. And last but not least, it's also a bit of a peer review, which is very powerful from several perspectives. It's funny how shy we all are about complimenting one another on a job well done, as though it's either embarrassing or it somehow makes us "less than" if we admit others are instrumental to the success of the organization. But when you set the stage that giving away the credit is the point of the exercise and you invite people to rise to that occasion, you and your team will be pleasantly surprised how much good energy and good will is generated!

To drive home the power of leaving your ego at the start line and the importance of utilizing all team assets for a collective success versus individual glory:

- Gather your team in a room and give them the following goal: "Learn and recite the alphabet backwards from memory. You have two minutes." Many people will instantly see this as a personal challenge and desire to be the solo act that pulls off an impressive feat—so you will most likely see people writing furiously or rushing to a quiet corner and plugging their ears so they can begin rote memorization. The person who can think outside the box and satisfy their ego with a team success, versus individual glory, will quickly count the number of people in the room, divide up the sections of the alphabet and have each person learn a small part so the mission can be accomplished against a nearly impossible deadline. This is a great way to show people that success is just as meaningful, and far more likely, when everyone carries a small piece of the load.

ELEMENT 8:

KINETIC LEADERSHIP

"A company is like a ship.
Everyone ought to be prepared to take the helm."
—**Morris Weeks**

We all know that every great team has an amazing leader. But the world's most consistently high-performing teams have amazing *leaders* (with an *s*), and the leadership role is kinetic. It changes all the time based on individual strengths, the team's needs and the situation in which the team is operating. A team is stronger if everyone is prepared to take the helm, especially if each team member has the emotional intelligence to lead based on need.

CHANGE LEADERS

An important part of leading a team from ordinary to extraordinary is understanding and embracing the difference between management and leadership. According to writer and consultant Peter

Drucker, "Management is doing things right; leadership is doing the right things."

Manager and leader are two completely different roles, although we often use the terms interchangeably. In my opinion and experience, here's the difference between the two: managers are facilitators of their team members' success. They ensure that their people have everything they need to be productive and successful; that they're well trained, happy and have minimal roadblocks in their path; that they're being groomed for the next level; that they are recognized for great performance and coached through their challenges. Conversely, a leader can be anyone on the team who has a particular talent, who is creatively thinking out of the box and has a great idea, who has experience in a certain aspect of the business or project that can prove useful to the manager and the team. A leader leads based on strengths not titles.

The best managers consistently allow different leaders to emerge and inspire their teammates (and themselves!) to the next level. For example, in our team's case, Ian Adamson was better in the paddling sections than anyone else. Neil Jones was best at navigating through tough terrain. John Howard was our best overall strategist. Ian Edmond was an incredible, unstoppable mountain biker. I was really good at managing the team, keeping everyone fed, getting sponsors and dealing with the race organizers. So although we only had one formal team captain (or manager), when that starting gun went off, everyone became a leader at some point based on his or her level of expertise, whoever was the least sleep-deprived, whoever was strongest at the time or whoever had the best plan.

When you're dealing with ongoing challenges and changes, and you're in uncharted territory with no means of knowing what comes next, no one can be expected to have all the answers or rule the team with an iron fist based solely on the title on their business card. It just doesn't work for day-to-day,

"THE BRIGHTEST STARS DON'T CREATE THE GREATEST TEAMS. THE GREATEST TEAMMATES CREATE THE GREATEST TEAMS."

normal operations. Sometimes a project is a long series of obstacles and opportunities coming at you at high speed, and you need every ounce of your collective hearts and minds and skill sets to get through it.

This is why the military style of top-down leadership is never effective in the fast-paced world of adventure racing or, for that matter, our daily lives (which is really one big, long adventure, hopefully!). None of us is as smart as all of us. I truly believe in Tom Peters's observation that the best leaders don't create followers; they create more leaders. When we share leadership, we're all a heck of a lot smarter, more nimble and more capable in the long run, especially when that long run is fraught with unknown and unforeseen challenges.

CHANGE LEADERSHIP STYLES

Not only do the greatest teammates allow different leaders to consistently emerge based on their strengths, but also they realize that leadership can and should be situational, depending on the needs of the team. Sometimes a teammate needs a warm hug. Sometimes the team needs a visionary, a new style of coaching, someone to lead the way or even, on occasion, a kick in the bike shorts. For that reason, great leaders choose their leadership style like a golfer chooses his or her club, with a calculated analysis of the matter at hand, the end goal and the best tool for the job.

My favorite study on the subject of kinetic leadership is Daniel Goleman's *Leadership That Gets Results,* a landmark 2000 *Harvard Business Review* study. Goleman and his team completed an in-depth three-year study with over three thousand middle-level managers. Their goal was to uncover specific leadership behaviors and determine their effect on the corporate climate, and even more interesting, each leadership style's effect on bottom-line profitability. Believe it or not, one of the outcomes from this research was the discovery that a manager's leadership style was responsible for thirty percent of the company's bottom-line profitability! That's far too much to ignore. Imagine how much money and effort a company spends on new processes, efficiencies and cost-cutting methods in an effort to add even one percent to bottom-line profitability, and compare that to simply inspiring managers to be more kinetic with their leadership styles. It's a no-brainer.

Here are the six distinct leadership styles that Daniel Goleman uncovered among the managers he studied, as well as a brief analysis of the effects of each style on the corporate climate:

- **The pacesetting leader** expects and models excellence and self-direction. If this style were summed up in one phrase, it would be "Do as I do, now." The pacesetting style works best when the team is already motivated and skilled, and the leader needs quick results. Used extensively, however, this style can overwhelm team members and squelch innovation.

- **The authoritative leader** mobilizes the team toward a common vision and focuses on end goals, leaving the means up to each individual. If this style were summed up in one phrase, it would be "Come with me." The authoritative style works best when the team needs a new vision because circumstances have changed, or when explicit guidance is not required. Authoritative leaders inspire an entrepreneurial spirit and vibrant enthusiasm for the mission. It is not the best fit when the leader is working with a team of experts who know more than him or her.

- **The affiliative leader** works to create emotional bonds that bring a feeling of bonding and belonging to the organization. If this style were summed up in one phrase, it would be "People come first." The affiliative style works best in times of stress, when teammates need to heal from a trauma, or when the team needs to rebuild trust. This style should not be used exclusively because a sole reliance on praise and nurturing can foster mediocre performance and a lack of direction.

- **The coaching leader** develops people for the future. If this style were summed up in one phrase, it would be "Try this." The coaching style works best when the leader wants to help teammates build lasting personal strengths that make them more successful overall. It is least effective when teammates are defiant and unwilling to change or learn, or if the leader lacks proficiency.

- **The coercive leader** demands immediate compliance. If this style were summed up in one phrase, it would be "Do what I tell you." The coercive style is most effective in times of crisis, such as in a company turnaround or a takeover attempt, or during an actual emergency like a tornado or a fire. This style can also help control a problem teammate when everything else has failed. However, it should be avoided in almost every other case because it can alienate people and stifle flexibility and inventiveness.

- **The democratic leader** builds consensus through participation. If this style were summed up in one phrase, it would be "What do you think?" The democratic style is most effective when the leader needs the team to buy into or have ownership of a decision, plan or goal, or if he or she is uncertain and needs fresh ideas from qualified teammates. It is not the best choice in an emergency situation, when time is of the essence for another reason or when teammates are not informed enough to offer sufficient guidance to the leader.

Now for the million-dollar question: which leadership style do you think was the most effective in creating a positive corporate climate and the greatest increase in bottom-line profitability, according to Goleman's research? When I ask this at my team building events, the predominant answer is pacesetting, which seems to reflect the way that many of us assume is the most effective way to lead. That is, get out front, lead the way and show 'em how it's done. But according to Goleman, the pacesetting style should be used very sparingly and with extreme caution. It is the antidote to team synergy and high morale because it doesn't allow individuals on the team to shine or have their turn in the spotlight. With a pacesetting style, the leader gets all the credit for being the hero whenever there are successes, and whenever there are failures, it's blamed on the team members' lack of motivation. When a leader spends too much time in a pacesetting role, employees often feel diminished, micromanaged and undervalued. Remember Ranger Boy, the team captain in the Fiji Eco-Challenge? Pacesetter all the way. He had to be the strongest, the person who knew the most and used his knowledge to control the team, and the person who would never acknowledge or give credit for the excellent ideas or performance of others. He destroyed his team in thirty-six hours. I'm sure we've all had a Ranger Boy in our lives at some point.

Now let's look at the other side of the coin: what did Goleman suggest was the most effective style that we live in most often as leaders? Authoritative. When a leader is a visionary who can inspire people to strive for an end goal and, most important, requests their help and input to get there, employees are motivated. They have a sense of entrepreneurship, and they definitely own the outcomes. It's the best-case scenario for a high-performance team.

A great example of success using the authoritative style was our team in the Tibet Raid Gauloises, when our mountain bikes and crew didn't make it to the final transition area. Robert, John and Keith provided a vision of how we as a team would see a challenge instead of a roadblock. They elevated our spirits by asking us if we could ride those local bikes and by giving us a way to still win by showing the world how the best team in the sport handles adversity. Within minutes, we had three strong leaders taking charge, one-hundred-percent ownership from the rest of the team (as our leaders gracefully invited us to rise to the occasion) and a higher sense of purpose that propelled us to the finish line against all odds. Choosing the right leadership style in that instant was critical, and our teammates hit the nail on the head. Without realizing it, they had naturally chosen the authoritative, democratic and affiliative leadership styles to help us manage our adversity, and it resulted in an incredible experience and an emotional "win" for us. If we had been told what to do or if one leader had attempted to victoriously get out front, take the credit and be the hero of the day, there would have been a mutiny.

Our top fire captains are masters at situational leadership. Because we are working as a family for twenty-four hours a day, ten days each month, the manager (captain) of the crew has to wear many hats and change them seamlessly, depending on the matter at hand. For much of the day, the most admired and respected fire captains employ an affiliative or democratic leadership style, both of which are very effective for "business as usual" operations. We share cooking, station maintenance and cleaning duties. We eat together, we work out together and we train together. In the afternoons, we generally do some kind of equipment or medical training, during which the captain switches to a coaching style. And when the alarms go off, and we are going full code with lights and sirens to a fire or traffic accident, it's time for a pacesetting style, which allows the captain to establish a command presence on scene and create a plan of attack that he then shares with the incoming crews. Then, last but not least, when it's crunch time and life-threatening events are happening all around us at an accelerated rate, the coercive style is the most effective tool. For safety's sake and to save patients' lives, we as the crew are often told, in no uncertain terms, exactly what to do and how to do it. And we wouldn't want it any other way. Bottom line? If you take two cups of authoritative leadership, one cup of democratic, coaching and affiliative leadership, and a dash of pacesetting and coercive leadership "to taste," and you lead based on need in a way that elevates and inspires your team, you've got an excellent recipe for long-term leadership success with every team in your life.

KINETIC LEADERSHIP:
A BUSINESS CASE STUDY

One company that used kinetic leadership to its distinct advantage was the Walt Disney Company. Launched as a small cartoon studio in Kansas City in the 1920s by brothers Walt and Roy, the company grew into a global icon not only because of Walt's renowned artistic genius but also because of Roy's understated, and largely unsung, financial savvy. While Walt and his animators were busy in the studio creating Mickey Mouse, Snow White, Cinderella and Sleeping Beauty, Roy was doing the unglamorous but essential work of securing the financing that allowed them to stay in business.

It wasn't easy for Roy to talk banks into taking a chance on his and his kid brother's fledgling studio, especially during the Depression and war years, and especially when no one really knew what the heck this animation stuff was all about. Roy and Walt became masters at tag-team leadership when it came to the banks: strait-laced businessman Roy would open the door by forging the initial relationship with the financial institutions, convincing the loan officers that he and the Walt Disney Company were legitimate and trustworthy; then the passionate visionary Walt would march in with his film canister full of magic, fire up the projector and seal the deal.

Walt and Roy's ability to defer to each other when it came to their respective areas of expertise was the key to their success. Neither could have built the company without the other. Walt once told a journalist, "Roy and I must have a guardian angel. We could never split up like Dean Martin and Jerry Lewis. Roy doesn't know whether it's my guardian angel, and I don't know whether it's his."[9] And listen to this testament to the power of kinetic leadership, from the ever humble Roy: "My brother made me a millionaire. Do you wonder why I want to do everything I can to help him?"[10]

SYNERGY STARTERS: KINETIC LEADERSHIP

To build your team by utilizing the unique strengths and talents of each team member:

Have each member of the team answer the following questions:

1. What talents or unique experiences do I have that can add value to my team (work- and non-work-related)?
2. What are some examples of how the team might benefit from my experience?

9   Bob Thomas, *Walt Disney: An American Original* (New York: Hyperion, 1994), 281.
10   Ibid., 284.

3. Some of my greatest business successes can be attributed to…

Once you have received and analyzed the answers, choose at least one talent/strength reported by each team member and set up a monthly "coach's corner" via conference call or videoconference, in which that month's "coach" prepares a ten- to fifteen-minute presentation designed to share their skill with the rest of the team for mutual gain. Some examples might be "how to train for a 10k" and set a goal as a team to run or walk a 10k on the same day (in respective cities), or "how I won the biggest bid of my career" or "a sales secret that works—from a former buyer in the industry." This empowers each team member to contribute as a leader and to feel even more responsible for the outcomes. Plus, it creates a great environment for mentorship and promotes deeper human connections and team synergy.

To assess and provide feedback on leadership strengths and weaknesses (among teams of peers or as a 360-degree analysis from employees):

For ten minutes, have each team member brainstorm about the specific behaviors and strengths of the best leaders/coaches they have had in their lives and conclude their session by compiling their "Top 5 Leadership Behaviors/Skills" list.

Next, on a whiteboard, write each team member's "Top 5 Leadership Behaviors/Skills." Cross out the duplicates and have the team build consensus (via votes) on which of those behaviors should be included in a general "Top 10 Leadership Behaviors/Skills" list.

Take the Top 10 list and have each team member write those behaviors down the left-hand side of the page. Then for peers, write the name of each leader in the room (other than yourself) from left to right across the top of the page. Pass the page around to each person in the room and have them report, on a scale of 1 to 10, to what extent they believe the person being evaluated displays those leadership behaviors listed vertically down the left margin. For example:

Evaluation for Amy Brody

	Mike	Susan	Rene	Scott	Average Score
Behavior 1					
Behavior 2					
Behavior 3					

For a 360-degree review or if you'd like for each of the peer evaluators to be anonymous, each employee/peer in the group can draw a number and report accordingly. For example:

Evaluation for Amy Brody

	#1	#2	#3	#4	Average Score
Behavior 1					
Behavior 2					
Behavior 3					

This kind of peer review and 360-degree feedback is always scary. But if feedback is offered with a positive spirit and accepted with the same, it's amazing how quickly you can become a better leader. Your employees *want* you to be a great leader and they want to respond positively to you. It's up to you to discover their needs and ensure you are fulfilling them.

To inspire situational analysis among your leaders/managers:

Order *Harvard Business Review* reprints of Daniel Goleman's "Leadership that Gets Results" (or at least put an annotated version together). Have your leadership team write down each leadership style at the top of a blank page and then have two columns underneath that say "utilize when" and "avoid when." Have them brainstorm individually about the situations in which each style should be utilized or avoided. After each team member has completed their lists, have an open discussion about when and where to use each style as it pertains to your particular business or industry (for example, integrating a sales force from a smaller competitor that your company just purchased or determining the best style to use in the final two weeks of a project with a tight deadline). Another dimension can be added to the discussion if your team prepares some real world "case studies" about their leadership challenges and the group discusses how those challenges might best be solved with a strategic choice of leadership style. The goal will be for your leadership team to realize how important and effective it is to use the right tool for the job at hand and not rely solely on "your style."

THE FINISH LINE

Wow, here we are gang! We're almost at the finish line—approaching the final stretch of this book together. This has been a crazy time, working on the book during flights to and from my keynote engagements and between calls at the fire station late at night. But you, dear reader, have been with me all along, and even though I was technically alone, I was always thinking of you and hoping you were going to enjoy being on my team for this journey. It's funny—despite the number of times I said I couldn't wait until I finished this book, now that the end is in sight I don't want to leave you, or have this adventure be over. So instead of rushing across the finish line, I'll tell you one more story. Then you can get on with your teambuilding life and maybe shoot me an email through my website every now and then about how amazingly happy and successful you are. That would make my day.

The tale of Team Eastwind is my favorite. I decided to finish this book with it because this team did every single one of the Eight

Essential Elements of Human Synergy so beautifully and gracefully; it was one of the most amazing team experiences I've ever witnessed. My team was having a terrible race at the 1997 Eco-Challenge, and we were just in front of Team Eastwind in twenty-second place. The only reason we knew that something noteworthy was going on behind us was because as we were trudging through the darkness on our way down Mount Bartle Frere, we turned a corner on the trail and BAM! The whole world was lit up like Times Square with television cameras and floodlights in our faces. I was so excited, thinking that the media still cared about us even though we were so far back in the field. I began preparing some off-the-cuff statements in my head for an interview, when suddenly the producer yelled, "Shut down! Shut it down! Don't waste batteries. It's not them," and the world faded once again to black. Reality check complete. It wasn't until the Eco-Challenge aired on the Discovery Channel that we knew the real story unfolding on the mountain behind us.

It was day seven when Japan's Team Eastwind, a four-person team that was still far behind in the pack, sought medical attention for their lone female teammate, Nahoko Hayama. Her ankle was swollen and painful; she had been limping in agony for hours when the team entered the transition area in the foothills of Queensland's Mount Bartle Frere.

In the medical tent, a race doctor delivered the devastating diagnosis: Nahoko had suffered perhaps the most serious and painful ankle injury there is, a torn Achilles tendon. Television cameras documented the drama as a stunned Team Eastwind heard the news.

"She's just not bending her foot at all, and you've got to get her over the tallest mountain in the state," the doctor told Nahoko's teammates. "It rises up to sixteen hundred meters (5,250 feet).... I honestly just don't think she's going to make it."

Team Eastwind knew that even if Nahoko were healthy, there was no way they would win the race because the winners had already crossed the finish line. Nevertheless, the team members were totally, insanely committed to completing what they had set out to do. They had trained so hard and come so far and sacrificed so much already. After a few moments of team deliberation, they decided that they would do whatever it took to complete the race—for one another, for their families and, most important, for Japan. No Japanese team had ever finished a major international adventure race. For Team Eastwind, this race now became a matter of national pride, a moment to show the true Japanese spirit of competition.

"The doctor said if we wanted to go on, we would have to carry her," one teammate said. "[Nahoko] asked us if we could do it, and we took that as a challenge. So I told her that, yes, we would carry her if necessary."

ESSENTIAL ELEMENT #1: **TOTAL COMMITMENT**

Even after the fun stopped, Team Eastwind showed total commitment, not only to the end goal of finishing the race, but also to one another and to their country. They had prepared and planned. They reached for a higher purpose (to show the "true Japanese spirit" of competition), and above all they were determined to persevere.

After a quick snack grabbed from the bottom of their muddy backpacks, the members of Team Eastwind mustered up their collective courage for the daunting task that lay before them: a perilous thirteen-hour hike up and over the highest mountain in Queensland, Mount Bartle Frere, which is entirely covered in thick, snarled rain forest from the foothills to the summit. Nahoko tried her best to walk, but it was a slow, agonizing death march for the team on that difficult terrain. She would take one step with her good left foot, dragging her practically useless right leg behind her; then take another tentative step and drag her right foot along again in a painful, lurching sidestep, consoled and encouraged by her three teammates, who never left her side. This continued throughout the long, cold night, inch by inch, foot by foot. Ascending through the jungle fueled by patriotism and team spirit, Team Eastwind was not going to give up without a fight.

ESSENTIAL ELEMENT #2: **EMPATHY AND AWARENESS**

Team Eastwind showed extreme empathy for their female teammate, whom they didn't treat as mandatory gear but rather as a valued member of the team. They were able to put themselves in Nahoko's little hiking shoes and empathize with how hard it was for her to be out of control and helpless, which bonded her to them and kept her in the game.

When the reporters inside the media helicopters spotted Team Eastwind at first light the next morning, only about a mile from the summit of Bartle Frere, they couldn't believe their eyes. Team

Eastwind was carrying Nahoko on their backs up the final pitches to the peak, steadily and patiently crawling, scrambling, clawing their way up the muddy, root-strewn track. They had been silently struggling like that for hours, alone, in the dark. But in the light of day, they were about to become international heroes. It was the most unbelievable physical feat ever seen in our sport: three small but mighty men alternately carrying a full-grown woman (well, the Japanese version of a full-grown woman; they're just glad it wasn't me!) on their backs up a nearly impassable, slimy, unbearably steep jungle trail.

"They have been carrying her on their backs for about six hours," reported the journalist watching the drama unfold from the helicopter hovering overhead. "She got off and with her walking stick was able to walk part-way, and they put her back on their backs when they got to another steep area."

ESSENTIAL ELEMENT #3: ADVERSITY MANAGEMENT

Team Eastwind managed their adversity by focusing on seeing a challenge versus a roadblock, and by having the collective mind-set to do what it took to win versus simply not lose, with the win being crossing the finish line together. They accepted their setbacks as a chance to show their determination and courage, and they most certainly never let the pursuit of perfection hinder their progress.

Throughout the climb, Team Eastwind looked for ways to stay engaged and make their difficult journey a little easier. One teammate came up with an alternative technique for carrying Nahoko, which his teammates were happy to consider and ultimately employ.

"Our teammate Suzuki had experience in mountaineering, and he suggested a method of turning a [backpack] inside out to help carry her on our backs," one teammate explained. "Once we practiced a bit, it became apparent that we would each have to carry her by our own individual strength. So we each tapped into our own stamina. Then it became a different kind of competition, like, 'Let's show the true Japanese spirit of competition!'"

The terrain became even more treacherous the higher the team climbed. Countless times, the teammate carrying Nahoko tripped and fell over the logs, boulders and vines that blocked his path. The rest of the team would quickly swarm around their friends to put them back on their feet, check them for injuries, offer reassurance and help them get back on their way.

ESSENTIAL ELEMENT #4: **MUTUAL RESPECT**

The mutual respect among the members of Team Eastwind was obvious. They were always shaking hands and congratulating each other, sharing "positive aluminum cans" that they will remember for the rest of their lives. They mentored one another unselfishly, acted like a team at all times (no matter how they felt) and believed in one another beyond reason, which inspired each team member to rise to the occasion.

"We have a proverb in Japanese that says, 'Once you fall, you are closer to death but not yet dead.' So I think this was a test for us to never give up, even under the toughest of odds," said one member of Team Eastwind. "I think that's the real spirit of the Eco-Challenge, that everyone has to come to terms with what the Eco-Challenge gives them. This is not our team spirit. It's the Eco-Challenge spirit."

It was mid-morning when Team Eastwind arrived at the twenty-sixth checkpoint of the race, the peak of Bartle Frere. They had achieved their interim goal of getting everyone to the summit, but their race was far from over. Between them and the launch point for the final sea kayaking leg to the finish lay a treacherous three-thousand-foot descent that took the best teams in the race over five hours to complete, followed by a thirteen-mile hike through the steamy mist of the sugar-cane fields in temperatures that exceeded one hundred degrees. The checkpoint officials warned the team captain that the way down was extremely steep, rocky and slippery, and asked the team if they needed medical help or if they wanted to continue.

"Keep going" was Team Eastwind's unanimous reply. "Keep going . . . yes!"

After allowing themselves a moment to celebrate when they reached the peak, Team Eastwind slowly headed downhill on the little trail that the other teams had blazed, steeled for the battle that they knew would take them into the cold, dark night . . . again. Within moments, they disappeared from the open peak into the jungle canopy. All afternoon, they carefully and slowly picked their way down the face of the mountain with Nahoko on their backs, slipping and sliding and crashing through the thick rain forest on their brave quest for level ground. Time and again, they fell from large boulders onto the jungle floor, crashing through the trees and skating down the death-defying mudslides left from the twenty-two teams that had already slithered down that same chute hours and days before. With nothing left for their shoes to grip, the only option was to slide from tree trunk to tree trunk, hanging on for dear life with Nahoko in terrified tow.

ESSENTIAL ELEMENT #5: **WE THINKING**

You know Team Eastwind was a We Thinking team by the fact that they operated as a colony of ants. Every single person took turns carrying Nahoko, while the other team members made sure that everyone had food, water and an endless supply of motivation. They did whatever it took. There was no comparing, competing or criticizing. If they succeeded, they all succeeded. If they failed, they all failed. They were taking everyone across the finish line together, and that was that.

When they finally reached flat ground at around midnight, the members of Team Eastwind were exhausted but thrilled. They had climbed the highest mountain in the state together, against all odds. They rewarded themselves with a three-hour sleep before their early morning push to the kayak leg. The camera crew caught up with the team early the next morning, slowly hiking through the cane fields and encouraging one another.

"Man, you did good yesterday," said one teammate to another as he patted him on the back. "Good job, my friend."

The men shook hands and laughed.

"Come on! *Vamonos, vamonos!*" one called good-naturedly over his shoulder to Nahoko, who was hobbling along a few paces behind them. "We've got to stick together!"

Nahoko's step quickened, and she smiled.

ESSENTIAL ELEMENT #6: OWNERSHIP OF THE PROJECT

Each teammate was determined to show the true Japanese spirit, which was a core value of each team member. The team also adopted a democratic leadership style, listening to and employing one another's ideas. They hired the inspired *and* inspired their hires along the way.

Throughout the long, painful march to Bramston Beach for the start of the final kayak leg, Team Eastwind, exhausted but determined, continued to take turns carrying Nahoko. Whenever one teammate was carrying her, the others walked beside him, picking up the shoulder straps on his backpack and taking some of the weight. The four of them were locked together in formation, like the Blue Angels flight squadron, for miles. One team, one purpose. Their legs were giving out, but their hearts were as one, beating in unison with an entire country. Imagine that level of motivation! They probably knew by now that their epic journey would be broadcast on television sets throughout the world and that they were not only representing their team but also honoring their country.

At one point, team captain Masato Tanaka was so sleep-deprived that he could barely function. But instead of asking the team to stop so he could sleep, he ran two miles ahead so he could lie down and have a fifteen-minute nap before carrying Nahoko again.

ESSENTIAL ELEMENT #7: **RELINQUISHMENT OF EGO**

The members of Team Eastwind were constantly giving away the credit to their teammates, as well as accepting all the help they could get from one another. It was interesting to me how not one of the males on the team stood out as the hero. None of them seemed to want or need that recognition. For Nahoko's part, she definitely had to leave her ego at the starting line in order to be carried. The team's goal was more important to her than her individual glory or how she appeared on camera. She gave her teammates the ultimate gift: she let them be her heroes.

Ironically, the flat road that they were so looking forward to as they bashed through the jungle held no reprieve. The stifling heat of the cane field, coupled with the hard, flat blacktop, was finishing the job of completely destroying their feet. All four of them were limping now. Huge blisters on the balls and heels of their feet caused searing pain with every step, but still none of them would stop. Mile after mile, Team Eastwind silently showed the world the meaning of courage as they reached far past the outer limits of human endurance in their quest to reach the kayaks together.

When they finally glimpsed the ocean, they discovered to their shock and surprise that the locals had already heard about their story and had turned out in droves to give them a hero's welcome. Overcome with the emotion of the last two days, Team Eastwind hoisted Nahoko onto their shoulders. The jubilant crowd surrounded them and walked with them the final half mile to the official checkpoint on Bramston Beach, where they gently set Nahoko down in the sand next to her kayak, victorious at last.

"Team Eastwind are the epitome of what Eco-Challenge really stands for," said race organizer Mark Burnett. "Most people couldn't even walk over Bartle Frere. For them to carry that woman over that entire mountain, it's incredible."

ESSENTIAL ELEMENT #8: KINETIC LEADERSHIP

Throughout the race, Team Eastwind used all six of Goleman's leadership styles. Whether they were coaching one another, forging even deeper bonds of friendship, forming a consensus about how to tackle a difficult section of the course or taking charge when life-threatening matters were at hand, the team's leadership styles and shifting roles were fluid and dynamic.

Team Eastwind showed us the beauty of getting through a worthy endeavor, and the art and power of human synergy, to do something so profound and amazing with your teammates, something you could never do alone. I love the way they put Nahoko on their shoulders as they entered the final transition area. They didn't come in saying,

"Look how awesome we are that we were able to carry Nahoko here!" Instead, through their unselfish actions, they said, "Look how amazing Nahoko is for letting us carry her!" For me, the greatest lessons from Team Eastwind's incredible odyssey are these: we don't reach the stars by standing on our teammates' backs; we reach them by putting our teammates on our shoulders. And we don't inspire our teammates by showing them how amazing *we* are, we inspire them by putting them on our shoulders and showing them how amazing *they* are.

Team Eastwind didn't cross the finish line first, but are they winners? Of course. Were they a world-class team? Absolutely. All world-class teammates understand that being a great team builder isn't always about crossing a finish line first or achieving huge, hairy, audacious goals. A team builder is who you are and, most important, what you consistently do. Are you always the person who is willing to share both your strengths and your weaknesses with your team? Are you consistently focused on creating synergy and finding the win-win solution with family, friends, colleagues and clients?

If I had to choose just one key takeaway that I wish for you to carry in your heart and mind as you close this book, it is this: wake up every morning and make the conscious decision to see a world full of teammates instead of a world full of competitors. That belief creates positive thought, and positive thought leads to the positive attitudes and behaviors that draw other like-minded, open, wonderful people into your life. It is these people, the members of the team that you have built, who will ultimately propel you up any mountain or through any valley in your day or, on a deeper level, your life.

Being a true team builder at heart is, I think, the most important skill a human being can have for long-term success and a fulfilling life. As is the case with any other skill, it is something that must be practiced consistently. If your mind is focused on an "us and them" world, find a way to change that to us and us. This is your choice, every minute of every day. Draw people to you by being the light for them and by showing them how amazing they are. Be the kind of person that others want to be like and be near. Be what is good about someone's day, and you will have a teammate—for a moment, for a project, for a lifetime.

The true test of who you have been as a team builder in your career and in your life will not necessarily be measured in your moments of triumph but in those moments when you falter. When you stumble on your way to that finish line, are you surrounded by an inspired group of people who will rush in to pick you up, put you on their backs and carry you over that mountain? And most important, will you let them?

At the end of this crazy, beautiful life, we may die alone, but I believe we truly live and reach our greatest heights together.

So here we are at the finish line, gang, which now that I think about it, is really the starting line for the rest of your lifelong adventure as a team builder. As we swiftly approach the back cover of this book and your adventure ahead as a world-class team builder, I'll share with you the last words my team and I say to one another at every starting line: "Stay safe, stay friends and go like hell" (in that order!). Thank you so much for spending these hours of your life with me. I am honored and humbled that you have allowed me to be a member of your team for a small part of your journey.

Now...5...4...3...2...1...GO!

YOUR EXTREME TEAMWORK GEAR BOX

A World Class Teammate always:

- Plans for the worst but hopes for the best.

- Helps to create a greater sense of purpose for the team.

- Perseveres against all odds, especially when the fun stops.

- Connects to the person before the point.

- Coaches versus criticizes.

- Strives to be the person who others want to work with and work for.

- Sees challenges versus roadblocks.

- Is ruled by the hope of success versus the fear of failure.

- Embraces adversity as a chance to learn and excel.

- Never lets the pursuit of perfection hinder progress.

- Showers the team with positive aluminum cans.

- Shuts down gossip within the team.

- Mentors unselfishly.

- Acts like a great teammate always, regardless of how he or she feels.

- Believes in his or her teammates beyond reason.

- Gives respect as a gift, not a grade.

- Is always trying to find a way to take his or her teammates across the finish line.

- Accepts responsibility for team success and failure.

- Accepts, acknowledges and appreciates teammates versus comparing, competing and criticizing.

- Seeks synergy everywhere, with everyone.

- Leaves his or her ego at the starting line.

- Asks for and accepts help—it's a gift to the helper.

- Remembers that heroism elevates one of us, but humility elevates all of us.

- Gives away the credit.

- Wraps his or her ego around team success rather than individual glory.

- Brings inspired people onto the team.

- Inspires teammates by letting them lead and asking for their input.

- Understands when to manage and when to lead.

- Allows leaders to emerge based on their strengths.

- Utilizes just the right leadership style for the job at hand.

TURNING INSPIRATION INTO REALITY

Throughout this book I have provided exercises for each of the eight elements of teamwork. Now it's your turn to create an action plan to implement what you've learned in *How Winning Works*. Getting those goals and visions out of your head and having them flow through your fingers and meet paper somehow makes them more real. On the following pages write down:

- 3 personal goals
- 3 professional goals
- 3 ways you're going to create more synergy with your family, colleagues and customers

Then take these pages (or a copy of them) and put them in your wallet, tape them to your dashboard, or place it anywhere else where you will see it on a regular basis. Today marks the start line of the exciting adventure race that is the rest of your life!

"Life is not a journey to the grave with the intention of arriving safely in a pretty and well-preserved body, but rather to skid in broadside, thoroughly used up, totally worn out, and loudly proclaiming, 'Wow, what a ride!'"

—Anonymous

ACKNOWLEDGMENTS

A million muddy, sweaty hugs to all of the teammates I've raced with, learned from, laughed and cried with, sang with, got towed by, picked leeches off of and won and lost gracefully with on life-changing journeys across the most barren and breathtaking places on earth. You are my heroes. You are amazing. You showed me who to be and how to be as a teammate and leader. I love you!

Many loud ear kisses to my dad, who lent his eagle eye, wordsmithing skills and anal-retentive copyediting abilities to this book on several occasions when I was cross-eyed and trying to find the right (and wrong) words! You are the best Board of Advisor a girl could ask for. Behind many a confident, happy, accomplished woman is a great daddy.

With much gratitude for my Jeff, the official Honey Bunny, who has been here, there and everywhere for thirteen years as our teams' "man behind the curtain," making us look like we know what we're doing and fixing small problems before they become big ones. We literally could not have done it without you.

A big woohoo to my Project Athena Goddesses/Gods, who make me believe that with love, synergy and the power of the human spirit (and enough ibuprofen!) all things are possible.

A big hug to my mom, stepmom and sisters who wouldn't believe it if they knew that I tell people that *they* inspire *me* with their strength and have made me stronger.

Thanks to my beautiful and talented Fire Girls on Engine 47 for sharing all of the unforgettable moments, the laughter, the ups and downs that we call "the greatest job in the world"! Working side by side with you every day for the benefit of others is a privilege and an honor. And thanks for trying to teach me to cook, too. Good effort.

And last but not least, a toast (and promised future happy hour) to the friends who believed in me and this crazy book, and who played an important role in making it a reality! Thank you for your patience and your guidance Deb Brody, Kris Verdeck, Amy Moore-Benson, Pamela Suarez and Christa Haberstock. And thank you, most of all, for seeing past the extreme to the sublime. We did it!!

INDEX

ABOUT THE AUTHOR

As a two-time world champion Eco-Challenge adventure racer and full-time San Diego firefighter, Robyn Benincasa knows a thing or two about creating human synergy, or as she puts it, "that magic that allows groups of ordinary people to accomplish extraordinary things together." She was a top-ranked sales representative (and rookie of the year) for a major pharmaceutical company for seven years before ditching her pantyhose for a backpack and some fireproof bunker pants. Since 1994, Robyn and her teammates have studied extreme teamwork in the most unique and compelling classrooms on Earth: the jungles of Borneo, the Himalayan peaks of Tibet, the rivers of Fiji, the rain forests of Ecuador and the epic brush fires of southern California. It is through these harrowing, life-affirming and often hilarious experiences in the world's most grueling challenges that she has emerged with her refreshing and unique perspective on what it takes to build the kind of world-class teams that succeed against all odds, triumph in the face of adversity and go the distance in any endeavor.

Since 2002, Robyn has also interviewed and consulted with hundreds of companies about their successes, strategies and challenges through her own team building consulting company, World Class Teams. Her teamwork presentations have inspired employees of dozens of major corporations, including Starbucks, Aflac, Fast Company, Siemens, 3M, Coldwell Banker, Ameriprise, Microsoft, ARAMARK, Nestlé, Hewlett-Packard, Four Seasons and Lincoln Financial Group.

Robyn founded the nonprofit Project Athena Foundation after undergoing hip replacement surgery in 2007, with the mission of helping other female survivors of medical or traumatic setbacks live an adventurous dream as part of their recovery. "Doctors can cure the body," Benincasa says, "but Project Athena cures the spirit."

Her accomplishments have been featured in dozens of media outlets, including NBC, ABC, CNN, ESPN, USA Network, The Today Show, Live with Regis, Dateline NBC, Discovery Channel, *Vogue*, *Sports Illustrated*, *Harper's Bazaar* and *Outside* magazine.